THE KEY TO FREEDOM

PERMANENT POWER OF LOVE OVER OPPRESSION

BETHANY HOLLINS

WESTBOW
PRESS®
A DIVISION OF THOMAS NELSON
& ZONDERVAN

Scripture taken from the King James Version of the Bible.

WestBow Press books may be ordered through booksellers or by contacting:

WestBow Press
A Division of Thomas Nelson & Zondervan
1663 Liberty Drive
Bloomington, IN 47403
www.westbowpress.com
1 (866) 928-1240

ISBN: 978-1-5127-5928-0 (sc)
ISBN: 978-1-5127-5929-7 (hc)
ISBN: 978-1-5127-5927-3 (e)

Library of Congress Control Number: 2016916710

Print information available on the last page.

WestBow Press rev. date: 10/20/2016

CONTENTS

ACKNOWLEDGEMENT PAGE

The Lord is my strength and my provision.

- Geovani Junior Jackson
- Nelson & Joan Brown

INTRODUCTION

Whenever someone comes up with a really good idea for a project, sometimes they only want particular people to know about it; And because they know that some people would be beneficial to the plan, but others would just mess it up or try to gain victory out of it, they hire people who would respect their layout and remain loyal. A plan that is so spectacular enough for everybody to enjoy would only work if those involved could keep in line with the work that they were called to do. The times of difficulties might break them down at first but if they followed it the right way and endured, it would make them capable of being built up better than before. People pick those whom they know are perfect for a specific task. Sometimes their children or relatives get picked to participate in the project so they know that everyone would all be on one accord.

Now they don't have to worry about people coming up with their own agendas for themselves. When people have a great plan to fufill God's task, most times problems will arise and try to get in the way. People will get doubted and criticized for it, even through persistence in trying to tell them that this is a good plan; some people (somewhere in their minds) think differently, and won't come to terms with the plan even when it is highly effective and beneficial. The question may arise "Does this person think they are better than me?" It could be that they don't like or are concerned with the approach since they don't understand the agenda. Due to a lack of trust, they could doubt or want to do something different and the list goes on; Nevertheless, this plan, is a Great one! Their children may begin to doubt but they keep going along with it out of love, and sometimes they try to come up with their own ideas to fit their own seperate agendas. How does this make the person feel? Well, If you said horrible, then imagine how God feels about His creation. The difference is that God is not stingy with His plan even though in the wrong hands it could be twisted and manipulated by men. He shares His love with everyone who wants to know Him. He loves us and He doesn't seperate Himself from us, we seperate ourselves from Him. There is so much to know about Adam and Eve and creation. Being intolerant to many things in life is constantly a frustration. It creates misunderstandings that only provokes the unlearned; But knowing God and following His plan is beneficial to all.

God is not impatient like us. He doesn't immediately cast us off, but instead He considers us His sons and daughters and builds a lasting foundational relationship with us, once we get to know Him. He tolerates us when we create our own plans aside from His. He suffers long with us and even pleads with us out of love for us & for our protection inside of His well kept plan. Once someone completes a mission, and has everything needed to maintain it, they usually don't continue with those that were contrary to the mission's progress but only wants to enjoy the fufilment out of it. They usually continue on in essence of celebrating and moving ahead in life. They don't want to be brought back down. Since God doesn't want us to perish even though we were contrary to Him and His plan for us, we still don't lack in being able to be part of His fufilment plan. Sometimes, what you know and have learned in this life, can be your worst enemy; but it is only when you rend your heart and mind to God, (laying aside what was learned by doctrines of men) that He can and will show you all things. Everyone still has a chance to be saved, they just have to believe it. As we can see now, so many of us have chance after chance to know truth, but we reject it because we value something more than we value Him. We have understanding or knowledge that exceeds the simple truths. The intellect that we are so fascinated about well, we got a chance to see the price we pay for obtaining it from the beginning, so why chase after it all over again? Maintaining heavy burdens all by ourselves has become easier in satans world. But those who do what is right will obtain everlasting life and peace.

God is a gracious and merciful God that doesn't want to make us bother ourselves about our own selfish pursuits; but when we come to know Him, He will show us the way. Like in times past, those things that were acceptable sacrifices are no longer acceptable to God anymore. They were only a shadow, until the time would come where Jesus would fufill ALL things. He wants to give us more than what pertains to this life. He wants to give us more than what we know and that is why the work is already laid out for us. He knows what we like. He knows our greatest fears and our greatest strengths. He is our father and He wants to bring us to completion in His way and process. Too often, many people want to reach to the top by the process that is over-processed but still under-done. He assures us that we will get to the top in the right way; by and through Him. But by ourselves, we are only climbing up a pedestal to fall right back down. Intelligence has increased and prospered, yet still, there is nothing new under the sun to A Mighty God! Too many things get our time because too many demands are neccessary to maintain so many functions of life when all the time, the antidote is one thing.

(SCRIPTURE Matthew 13:15-17)
"For this people's heart is waxed gross, and their ears are dull of hearing, and their eyes they have closed; lest at any time they

should see with their eyes, and hear with their ears, and should understand with their heart, and should be converted, and I should heal them. But Blessed are your eyes, for they see: and your ears, for they hear. For verily I say unto you, that many prophets and righteous men have desired to see those things which ye see, and have not seen them; and to hear those things which ye hear, and have not heard them" ~Matthew 13:15-17

PROLOGUE

Xi "The story of Moses and the Egyptians"

(SCRIPTURE Exodus 2:24) "And God heard their groaning, and God remembered his covenant with Abraham, with Isaac, and with Jacob. And God looked upon the children of Israel, and God had respect unto them."

From this, we see how it was Moses' destiny given by God for him to leave out of Egypt and go into a land that he knew nothing about. In God's mercy upon His people, He knew the heart of Moses, and He knew exactly what he would do in his unsettled situation. We saw it too, how he smote the egyptian for mistreating a slave.

(SCRIPTURE) Exodus 2:12 Kjv "And he looked this way and that way, and when he saw that there was no man, he slew the Egyptian, and hid him in the sand."

That probably wasn't the first time he saw the mistreatment of slaves, (considering the constant injustice and cruelty of the the Israelites by the Egyptians during that time.)

(SCRIPTURE) Exodus 1:8-10 Kjv "Now there arose up a new king over Egypt which knew not Joseph. And he said unto his people Behold, the people of the children of Israel are more and mightier than we: Come on, let us deal wisely with them; lest they multiply, and it come to pass, taht, when there falleth out any war they join also unto our enemies, and fight against us, and so get them up out of the land. Therefore they did set over them taskmasters to afflict them with their burdens. And they built for Pharaoh treasure cities, Pithom and Raamses.

But maybe at that moment Moses couldn't bear to see anymore hardship on the people. On His journey away from what he called home, he began a new destiny but little to his knowledge, God had a bigger plan for him to bring His people out of bondage. Now it was at the time Moses was tending his flock of sheep when he was called to a bush of flaming fire. And God intervened the Angel to speak to him, and commanded him to go back his homeland that he left and to save His people from out of the hand of the Egyptians. Can you imagine how he must have felt? He must have been in Awe, afraid, excited, maybe even concerned about his task. Well, it is written, that he was scared as ever. Then to hear the voice of God? So now to do such a Mighty work back in his own hometown where he would have been killed? But God's voice was MIGHTY, so I'm sure he knew that he didn't have much of a choice; And God not only trained him for his journey, but was going before him all the way. God could have even been training Him for his mission to lead during the time he was tending the sheep. Many people saw that Moses was a strong man in which he was. He completed the call that God placed on his life. He was modest about it and must not have seen it in that way because he had trouble facing the call. In asking God for help, God gave him his brother Aaron to go alongside him, and to speak for him those things in which God commanded him to say to pharaoh; but God was displeased by him not wanting to speak.

The scriputure references to these statements can be found in Exodus 3:1, Exodus 6:12 Exodus 7:1 and 2 out of the KJV Bible. We all have our times when it is up to us to completely trust in

God and have faith for the calling He places on our lives. We hear His voice living in these times too, and we have to react to the call placed on our lives. God can reach us when we have our hearts in the right places, He can restore us from past sins and set us free when we simply make the choice to turn completely to Him from sin. And though we may mess up in following Him, He stretches out His hand to lift us up and He tells us to keep going. As long as we desire Him, He will keep us. We have a choice.

(SCRIPTURE 1 Chronicles 22:19) "Now set your heart and your soul to seek The LORD your God; arise therefore, and build ye the sanctuary of the LORD God, to bring the ark of the covenant of the LORD, and the holy vessels of God, into the house that is to be built to the name of the LORD."

This is a commandment from God Himself to set our hearts to seek Him. In the specific task He gives us, we know that we are able to complete it because He is our help. Moses was raised in a rebellious Nation that did things contrary to the truth of God and His Word. Though he was born an Isrealite, he was raised a prince in Egypt and he knew the corruption of that place very well, and the heart of the people who lived there. He could have been born a slave with the Isrealites, but his divine purpose was to bring the people of God out of bondage from that physically oppressed place. We can reflect the same image in this day and age here in the United States. There are people that God has chosen, to bring our Nation out of the bondage from mental oppression and slavery of the mind. All around the world people are being oppressed for loving the true Word of God and not conforming to society's ways. Unfortunately corruption of society takes place in the midst of people beginning to trade character over for the things of this world. With purpose, things that are hard to take in, are said, but frustrating topics get un-frustrating and those who wait, usually find out the foundation of messages when they have patience. Whenever a person wants to do something good, evil is always present with them. The nature in our being shows this, though from the beginning it wasn't so. Now, our corrupt nature in our mind is being abused even moreso due to society's "need for more". Our definition of love can only be partial. It can never be pure or set-apart without God's divine love and intervention. God is just and is merciful! Since Moses made the choice to flee from the wrath of the king, when he could have made peace offerings with him and just continue to settle in that place with it's luxury and fine delicacies, he stepped out in an act of faith, as percieved by God. He took a stand and he heard the voice of God.

(SCRIPTURE Hebrews 11:27 KJV) "By faith he forsook Egypt, not fearing the king: For he endured, as seeing Him who is invisible"

When God wants to do a Mighty work, that mighty work begins in the work of the heart of man. But when our hearts are constantly in the wrong place not willing to do right, then how can we allow God to pour out His grace on us? God is merciful, and even if Moses' heart wasn't completely in the task prior to smiting the egyptian, It later began to be towards his departure. This act of faith was what God counted as acceptable. In like manner, our acts of faith following Jesus, show as well that we love not our lives unto the death.

(SCRIPTURE Revelation 12:11 KJV) "And they overcame him by the blood of the Lamb, and by the word of their testimony; and they loved not their lives unto death"

LIES OF THE ENEMY

You are not in bondage to a self-made form of love that evaporates overtime, but you have the power to be transformed by true love. Religion comes by tradition which can in turn seperate someone from the true love of God. Jesus addresses exactly what He considers pure "Religion" in James 1:27.

(SCRIPTURE James 1:27 KJV) "Pure Religion and undefiled before God and the Father is this, To visit the fatherless and widows in their affliction, and to keep himself unspotted from the world."

These are considered natural and common things to do but they have been pushed aside because of a rushed society. Mercy and truth have been forsaken in this land along with the knowledge of God, to form a new seemingly peaceful way of life while here on earth; but it cannot stand without the operation of God. He will condone those things that are from Him and operated by Him. There is no new knowledge, but because of a selfish society, the morals and minds of men are constantly corrupted just to fit the selfish pursuits of man; People's basic needs have multiplied, due to the increasing number of circumstances ... Due to the circumstances, Jesus was cruicified. Due to the circumstances, those who passed over one helpless man on the side of the road weren't accounted worthy to be called a "Good samaritan", even though through the eyes of man, they were called a priest. religion is made due to man's circumstances of not willing to submit to truth, and in turn creates a seperation. Seperation of mankind should always be examined from God's point of view because though we can seperate ourselves physically, we are all still under the authority of God, He made us! God shows us His seperation of mankind is by obedience vs. disobedience, (Looking at scripture as a whole). The tower of babel is one big incident that shows us how the seperation of man comes through disobedience. The seperation of man comes by the work of the flesh. It happens when man disobeys God and when he tries to get to God by his own way.

He also says …

(SCRIPTURE Matthew 25:31-34 KJV) "When the Son of man shall come in his glory, and all the holy angels with him, then shall he sit upon the throne of his glory: and before him shall be gathered all nations: and he shall seperate them one from another, as a sheperd divideth his sheep from the goats: and he shall set the sheep on his right hand, but the goats on the left. Then shall the King say unto them on his right hand, Come, ye blessed of my Father, inherit the kingdom prepared for you from the foundation of the world:"

And now the new religion is how you yourself can become a god. One of satan's devices in the last days. satan got cast down for that very reason and tries to entice a disobedient mind which is already programmed to corruption, and lure a mind to perform the evil desires of our carnal heart, but we are free from sin! God tells us how He will give us a new heart and spirit. You are not in bondage to a self-made form of love or religion! I'm not talking as a motivational speaker, but because you were specifically and specially designed to be you and only you can do it, you now have the freedom to pursue true love. We were given dominion over the world for proper maintenence, love and everything good, but through the bondage of corruption bought on by sin and disobedience, we now have to undergo a process of elimination. The corruption is so deep and the hurt of God's people is so drastic, now we simply can't come out of it on our own. Now, there is an inummerable amount of sin increasing overtime that only The Holy Spirit can guide us and lead us out of, according to our individual lives. Somewhere along the lines when we decide that it is up to us to pursue what we consider to be true love, we only end up at the starting point again. Every man can tally up their own definition of love according to their personal situations in life. The thing about that is we start to build a huge paradox and list of things that every man can't add up to be. So the result of every religous or traditional type of love always results in a sacrifice of some sort. Some require a sacrifice of man-kind even, because of dissaproval of religion and what they consider an "overpopulation". But God has built a distinct and unique form of love aside from tradition and things that not everyone can do. It's something we can do, absolutely every one of us! Once we look for God, leave sin, and ask for Jesus to come into our hearts, then we start the beginning of our process and walk with God.

If we begin to pursue anything with quality in which we are serious about, we find out sooner or later that the vision may start to seem blurred along the way. Although, it is possible to eliminate the tiresome things that we face when our hearts are indwelt in the project/ thing. It is the same way in our walk of getting to know God. We can't obtain His love by grabbing our own formula and mixing in a little bit of this and a little bit of that and that makes us happy, there! We can't get it by our own means because that's not neccessary or possible with the amount of people in the world that have their own uniqueness and different characteristics about them. In the Bible, and also in a religous book, you will find that in the beginning, it is written (SCRIPTURE Genesis 1:26 KJV) "Let US make man in OUR image".

Well that (US) means a whole lot! God The Father, Son and Holy Spirit, ONE GOD, referring to Himself (as He made us Body soul spirit/ one being). He saw us and reached out to save us from our corrupt nature. So, we are made after the image of God and we know even through science how that our mind and body communicates within itself by God for us to move, let alone for us to breathe. Through prayer and looking at that simple truth is how we can get an understanding of who God is, but only a relationship with God gives us a deeper knowledge and understanding of Him, and of ourselves.

(SCRIPTURE Romans 1:20 KJV "For the invisible things of him from the creation of the world are clearly seen, being understood by the things that are made, even his eternal power and Godhead; so that they are without excuse.

Even His eternal power and Godhead are seen by the things that are made, but to be perfect according to man's standards and to trust in one's own self, makes a person have to audit who they are, and to transform into something they're not, just to obtain being someone they weren't designed and can't permanently uphold to be.

It's called a masquerade. And even when they can manage it, they face the reality of it simply not being themselves. With the benefits that one reaps, the void is still deep. Once you know love, it puts you at liberty & ease to know that you are free from the bondages of self-justification or proving yourself, you and all others will know exactly who you are. You are free from work, stress, marriage, responsibility, children, partnership business etc. It's not made hard for us to get to that reality but, we make it hard on ourselves. We all may seek success at some point, but know that our success, (giving all thanks to Our Lord and Savior Jesus), comes from the minute we came out of the womb and was given a chance at life.

Our hardship gives us the ability to walk through the rain with a smile on our face and that then determines our progress in the future. We all want to reach our destination. Dancing in the rain makes it easier and the storm wont bother us, and may actually be the provision for our destiny. But it won't be by our own work to dance in the rain, because we know and keep our eyes on what He did. With one purpose, He showed us His great love for us! The only history we need to know is the history of who we are in Christ Jesus as He relates to each and every single person.

Even if you didn't know Him in past times or don't, you can still be a canidate for His Kingdom and God even has a special place for you in His word and works. We may not fully know why we continually associate our impure hearts with love, or why we can place the two together, but have you ever thought that God's love may not come from our very own hearts? We as human beings often seek for an "inner peace" to comfort us while we go on our daily lives. The problem is that, the inner peace we seek can never be filled in the right way when we only want to settle for the wrong impure way.

(SCRIPTURE Jeremiah 29:13 KJV) "And ye shall seek me, and find me, when ye shall search for me with all your heart.")

We all need and desire our inner peace. Sometimes we get a quick fix peace; a cup of coffee for a busy day. Someone at work makes you upset but then you remember your yoga and kick boxing appointment when you leave work and it helps you work out your frustration. But where is our way of peace coming from? Is it a type of peace that we must subdue it with another force of energy that overpowers that one. If someone has work that requires them to think alot and they need to drink coffee every morning, they drink it because it gives them peace for that moment. Now lets say oneday the coffee machine is down at work so they wait until there lunch break to run to mcdonalds and get a cup, but once they get there, the mcdonalds coffee is out of order, so they decide to go to 7 eleven and get one there but the machines are also down there. The person realizes that there time is up before they need to go back to work and take care of some major things. So this person (while back at work) decides to grab some candy to take place of that. Now, they have a candy habbit, and this is how we can start to build bad habbits for ourselves. Whether consciously or subconsious, we are always building. But it helps us when we consciously build in the right way. Even children can build for themselves and become a product of their own pursuits. When they are full grown, sometimes they maintain a foundation of what they build in their youth. The reality becomes, Are we building for ourselves and in the right way? When children do it, we can show, help and correct them. When we build for ourselves, we, by nature get shown, helped and corrected too. Even through society we are taught that we can't make other people happy unless we are happy first..In like manner, we can't be content in life enough to build ever-lasting foundations unless we are developed in our relationship with God. The buildings that we build for ourselves are costly, expensive and need the maintenence that temporary sources can provide.

Through the chastisement of God, we are able to see how we are governed by Him, because even though sometimes we may not feel like it, we are still living under His love and supervision. When we go out of His way to make a way for ourselves, sadly society can assist in making those efforts a reality so there are builders building for a temporary cause. The reality is that we are susceptible, even in churches; so our help in knowing the truth ultimately comes from above … When following the right way, we can still become a victim of our own selves because of our nature; but God always makes a lasting, filling provision when we're building up in His way, through faith. The other way always seems easy, because we get comfortable in the flesh. But when it comes to going a way that we don't know; we doubt, we nag, we complain and we have trouble keeping our eyes focused along the journey. We don't have to do anything by our own works when we reach the provision that God has for us, but by the works given through The Holy Spirit, and the words of the Scriptures. If God has a work set out for you, you must first know it, then you must pursue it. It is the only guarunteed work that was very costly, expensive, but doesn't need alot of maintenence in the way that we think it does. It will uphold us for a lifetime.

(SCRIPTURE "Be not afraid of their faces: for I am with thee to deliver thee, saith the LORD." Jeremiah 1:8 KJV)

THE "12" CHRIST'S DISCIPLES

God called 12 Disciples and chose them to witness and write down His Word, towards the closing of the written Word of God. Christ, called each of them out, from among their physical responsibilities to take on the spiritual duty of following Him; and He told them to "Follow Me". He lets us know in Luke 9:61-62 that if we are settled here, then how can we take on the spiritual responsibility of follwing Him in these last days. It says (SCRIPTURE Luke 9:61-62 KJV) "And another also said, Lord, I will follow thee: but let me first go bid them farewell, which are at home at my house And Jesus said unto him, No man, having put his hand to the plow, and looking back, is fit for the kingdom of God.")

The times where we can't even think without needing to constantly pray hard; The times where it is absolutely neccessary to put on a fast if you are following Christ.

Where knowledge, mercy and truth have been forsaken;

By examining these present last days, we can see how the world is getting further from truth. We might also witness some of the same experiences that the 12 encountered, while were walking with Christ on our journey. They all followed and strove to become like Christ. Though these all may have struggled with different challenges through their personalities. They are our guide and we may be able to reflect some of our characteristics through the individual experiences they encountered with Jesus. Thomas wouldn't believe that Jesus was seen by the disciples unless he was able to see the scars on His hands, put his finger into the print of the nails, and put his hand into His side. We know that our carnal (against God), fleshly character and attitude, deal with the struggles we encounter on our walk as a devout Christian. In our pursuit to attain Godliness, we conflict with the evil nature of our being that we are coming out of, but God helps us.

(SCRIPTURE Ephesians 6:12 "For we wrestle not against flesh and blood but against principalites against powers, against the rulers of the darkness of this world, against spiritual wickedness in high places." KJV)

We all want to be close to God right? To love and to know and to know God is to know and love His Only begotten Son. From time to time we all feel a little unconfident about ourselves. As satan tries to trigger our emotions and have us to rely on our feelings, we know that we are more than conquerors, because we don't wrestle against the flesh but against powers that we have little knowledge about so by His authority we are sustained. You may have heard the term "Mind over matter", well that term can be viewed in a Christian's perspective and walk. And when it is constructed in the right way it will reap eternal benefits. When our minds are constructed after Jesus, we can attain life. God wants us to be constructed in the only way possible to attain life, goodness, and true peace. Part of the problem as is again, that society takes bits and peices of truth to construct their own ideas and agendas into play; They have been placed together to be a puzzle peice a-part from God. In reality, nobody has the whole truth except God.

(SCRIPTURE1 Corinthians13: 9-10 KJV) Tells us "For we know in part, and we prophesy in part. But when that which is perfect is come, then that which is in part shall be done away with."

This scripture doesn't just limit to us believers in The Lord, this is for everyone in the world. We all know parts of the truth because All knowledge and power is given from God. The problem is when doctrines become a foundation for reality rather than the simplicity of loving and trusting in God with all of our hearts. We fail Him each day because we can't please God by means of the flesh. No not one person.

(SCRIPTURE Romans 8:7 KJV) "Because the carnal mind is enmity against God for it is not subject to the law of God neither indeed can be"; We get beside ourselves in thinking that we can please Him when we do good. Faith pleases God, God took away that burden from us many years ago of trying to please Him in the flesh through our vain sacrifices and good deeds.

(SCRIPTURE Romans 10:4 KJV) "For Christ is the end of the law for righteousness to every one that believeth."

UNDERSTANDING LOVE, DOES LOVE COME FROM OUR HEART

What it means to love, and our heart ... Those two simply can't be associated when looking at it in God's point of view. In (SCRIPTURE1 John 4:16 KJV)

We see that God is love. If we love mankind with our own heart, then how can we know the true love of God? Funny right? Well, He is love and our hearts are desperately wicked it says in (Jeremiah 17:9) The Holy Spirit lets us know that our carnal heart and mindset cannot please God, so that is why He has to come and renew it. How does He renew it? by changing it to His! We see His heart when we reach out and love others, our heart, when it wants to do something good, is the pure heart of God. He is impartial, we are partial in our hearts. Deciet brought us into the bondage of corruption by satan, like so, we are all still susceptible. So we must get rid of our carnal heart.

(SCRIPTURE Ezekiel 36:26 KJV) "I will give you a new heart and put a new Spirit in you; I will remove from you your heart of stone and give you an heart of flesh."

So then how can we love? Love is an action & Jesus tells us that there was no greater love than for a man to lay down HIS life for His friends. He is referring to Himself. He lets us know that we too (once recieving His heart) have the ability to do the same thing because He puts His Spirit in us, making us capable of doing All things. We know that once we have given our life to Jesus, we are no longer in bondage to sin and we no longer live for ourselves.

Love is an action, whether it be a spiritual, physical, or maybe even verbal one. It's not the anticipation of our next move that shows love when we have it in our power to do it, but the move in itself. We are incapable of fully loving by ourselves without the help of our Savior. So what we anticipate in our hearts to do for others when we can, we show love by our actions. He shows us that faith alone without works is dead. Somebody had a desire to help his friend carry in his groceries in when it was in his power to do so and yet he did nothing. The good samaritan stopped on the side of the road to offer help to the one who had gotten beaten by robbers after a priest and a levite walked by him with the desire to help. Understanding that God knows all things, our love can only be partial without knowing His love and guidance. He must work in us and He counted our very own belief on Him, to be considered worthy for our love because believing on Him is eternal. So likewise, our faith will allign with our works.

He tells us if we love Him we will keep His commandments.

(SCRIPTURE Proverbs 4:23 KJV) "Keep your heart with all diligence; for out of it are the issues of life."

When we put on the sheild of faith, it blocks out every dart from the enemy. We place it over our chest so that as we walk foward, these things in life that come our way, will hit the sheild and miss us. Our carnal man can be subdued through striking down fiery darts of lies and manipulation; and we know that faith is in

The Word. Faith comes by hearing it, and satan tries to make us put that same faith into what the world has to say or even into ourselves and other people, rather than in God. Well it is easy to be influenced when we hear what the world has to say; but when we believe God for what He says and that He is our sheild, we gain victory and confidence over our hearts. Only then is it easy to trust that a heart was truly rended to The Lord by the time circumstances hit. Our faith in Jesus is the most important thing in this world so if we allow things or circumstances or people into our hearts, how can we fully operate in the Will of God? By the fruits of the spirit, we know we love God, and when we love God, we know we love people.

(SCRIPTURE Mark 12:30 KJV) "And thou shalt love the Lord thy God with all thy heart, and with all thy mind and with all thy strength: this is the first commandment. And the second is like, namely this, thou shalt love thy neigbour as thyself. There is none other commandment greater than these."

Sometimes when we go through things, we want to share it with people. It's not always a bad thing but when you share, (or have shared things with let's say your parents for example), what usually happens is they try to fix the problem. The same thing goes when you have a husband, sometimes he tries to fix the problem rather than just listen to you when you just want a listening ear. You may already have a solution to the problem but you just want to talk about it. Anybody who wants a good foundational relationship with someone will learn that sharing is good at times, but when you share too much with someone, they start to form opinions about what you go through and so you find out that it may be specifically for you to not share. When we go through things with people, we may even get a quick answer or solution, but we always get limited information. But when we go through things with God, pouring our hearts out with Him, He not only gives us the answer we wanted (as we see in life sometimes later on), but it is guarunteed to fix the problem and He tells us the right things. He lets us know all things in our walk. Information given from the Holy Spirit through people is always right for you when given to you by God; but there is a difference between the flesh and the spirit. Submitted to God, there is always guaraunteed answer. Those in sanctification have the best listening ears.

God, oneday at work came and told me that "I'm not righteous", and I didn't fully understand what He meant by that at the time. I had an idea of what He was telling me but I didn't have the full understanding of what He meant. He meant your thoughts are not my thoughts and your ways not my ways, He is spiritual, I am carnal. He is good I am not. We have His Holy Spirit in us and we are to make use of what He entrusts to us, because we were bought with a price. He was telling me this and I couldn't fully grasp it's meaning until oneday about 6 months later, I realized that this was what He was telling me. The part in us that wants to do good is of God.

The part of us that wants to do bad is the work of the flesh which is corrupt by nature. We have a carnal mind and a spiritual mind in which we wrestle with, but the carnal mind is at enmity with God. If I want to be a physical person and see things through the natural eye, God might want to show me something that can only be seen through the spiritual eye. A long time ago, God revealed to me that everything with a physical nature also has a spiritual nature behind it, unless it is dead. Just because we see it now, does not mean that it won't at some point be extinct. Everything is real, but not everything is alive. If I go on a vacation in my mind, it is actually happening in my imagination and can be brought to life through a visual perspective, such as a movie. So while it is real and actual, if it has nothing to do with everlasting substance, it is considered dead because it will be extinct. We are capable of re-creation up to a certain point. If something is alive, then it will never be extinct. Our God has a complete set of instructions and divine order for how He does things just like this life. The difference is, His order is Holy.

(SCRIPTURE Romans 13:1-2 KJV) "Let every soul be subject unto the higher powers. For there is no power but of God: the powers that be are ordained of God. Whosoever therefore resisteth the power, resisteth the ordinance of God: and they that resist shall receive to themselves damnation."

(SCRIPTURE 1 Peter 2:13 KJV) "Submit yourselves to every ordinance of man for the Lord's sake: whether it be to the king, as supreme; Or unto govenors, as unto them that are sent by him for the punishment of evildoers, and for the praise of them that do well."

Sometimes, those Authorities go against God's order. There is a time and a season for everything says in Scripture Ecc3 KJV, and we know how it has been prophesied of one who would come and change the times and the laws

SCRIPTURE Dan 7:25 KJV It is such a good thing to know how we then become justified through the Spirit and not the letter. When God is alive in us, and our hearts are rendered to Him, we are walking with God and will watch ourselves so that we will not go out of His rightful order. Where there is a scripture to judge and to prove, there is also another scripture to balance and show the mercy of God, and how mercy rejoices against judgement when you're following God. We worship in Spirit and in truth. His Holy Spirit is poured out on us for us to do the work he tells us to do. Sometimes people think that it is by themselves or by there own effort; but we justify ourselves in our partiality. Doing good is only done by the hand of God, and not man, and we can never be perfect by ourselves, or form our own man instituted peace as the governing authorities have done and still do in this day.

(SCRIPTURE 1 The 5:3 KJV) "For when they shall say Peace and safety, then sudden destruction cometh upon them, as travail upon a woman with child; and they shall not escape."

Are we good? No.. That might be a hard saying when we wanna be right but All perfection and peace comes from God our Creator of All things!

Nothing we do can make us good, not our dressing not our or make up, but even in a sense of taking it off ... We are not justified by our own works. We walk in them as lead by Christ because He is our shield.

It makes us feel good to do or be "good" but it is God's Spirit moving within us; if it were not for Him and were reliant upon us, we wouldn't do good because it's easier to do bad; but Thank Him for His Holy Spirit that allows the good to rotate onto us. At such a corrupt time as this, where mercy is rarely shown and people have neglected the truth of God's Word to form a one world religion, God is still moving in the hearts of men to get them to do the right thing and to trust Him for the sacrifice He gave us. (in which any religion made by man will still require sacrifice in order for everyone to be on one accord,

As long as people are alive, they still have a chance to be forgiven and that is the beauty of Jesus! For it is written (SCRIPTURE

1 Corinthians 15:50 KJV) "Flesh and blood will not inherit the Kingdom"

We all make efforts to be comfortable in our flesh, but our time-span is short on earth and we don't realize it. Unfortunately sometimes, so is our perspective (SCRIPTURE 2 Peter 3:8 KJV) "But beloved, be not ignorant of this one thing, that one day is with the Lord as a thousand years, and a thousand years as one day."

God teaches us to want for nothing in this life, while this life teaches us to want everything our 5 senses desire. Well, why does God teach us to want for nothing when He made everything here for us? To fully know, we understand the sinful nature of man. Before the fall, God did want us to have everything in this world, and all things were pure. After the fall, we became impure. So while we are being made new, through the power and work of God, nothing becomes impure again to us just like before, and we then can truly inherit all things. Therefore while nothing here is for us, All things are for us.

WHEN OUR HEART IS IN THE WRONG PLACE

When the world teaches you how to be built up on yourself rather than how to pursue the call that God placed on your life, one of the hardest things to do is to come out of what we know. Once we learn what we think we know of ourselves, it's hard to change our minds from the things we are used to. Jesus warns us that who or what we set our affections or hearts on will be the place where our treasures reside so if we place our hearts on ourselves, that's exactly what we will be full of; (You may have heard of the term "Don't be full of yourself). The thing about it is we all wanna do right, but if we were perfect, we would make absolutely no mistakes. None of us are perfect. So let's say you set your heart on a person. Then all of your treasures will reside within that person, in which no man alone is capable of satisfying you completely without the work of God. So let's say that they are following the Spirit of God in them. Does that then make it okay for you to set your heart on them? No, because your heart still resides in that person and not in God. Since our hearts are imperfect, we can only trust the heart of God as we entrust the heart of man. One of those good pictures that I saw floating by on facebook was one of this couple kissing the Bible, with the Bible in between the two and both of them crying. My perception of that image is, that they have both come to the knowledge and understanding that they need God as their God & not eachother. They both put God first.

I think one misconception that we all can get is that we can love God and people on the same level. Well the first commandment is to love God with all of our heart mind and soul that doesn't limit us to some of our heart. Other scriptures tell us to trust no man.

SCRIPTURE 1 John 5:2 KJV "By this we know that we love the children of God, when we love God and keep His commandments."

This is what we have to do, love and keep His commandments.

God says to guard our hearts with all diligence but giving our heart to a person or thing is subconsciously trusting in them and reaping their fruits, that is why relationships don't last.

See (Proverbs 23:26 KJV)
Here is the Scripture where God proves how our love is by our actions towards the things He entrusts us with …

See (2 Kings 5:14 KJV)
A capitan of the host of the king of Syria named Naaman was told by the prophet Elijah by God that he would be healed of his leprosy if only he would go down into the Jordan and wash 7 times, but he got mad and said no & left because Elijah wouldn't honor him in the greeting that he wanted. Upon his departure, it was only through the persuasion of his servants that he was convinced to go back and do what the prophet told him so that he could be healed. So he did as Elijah told him and dipped in the water, then he was healed. That shows us how pride can lead to destruction if we don't repent. If he had not went and washed in that Jordan, he would have not been healed because of his pride. Jesus comes to us through seeking Him with our whole heart. He says if we seek Him, we will find Him if we seek Him with our whole heart. Naturally throughout the day our heart and

mind tends to get entangled with useless things called "junk". Whether it be a parfume or cologne we are thinking about, a new dress or even something as simple as food; Our next meal … But God intercedes for us when we give all of these things in our hearts that we have stored up, to HIM! He refreshes us with new thoughts that draw us closer and closer to The Kingdom, and our treasures soon become things that will not perish (Eternal Treasures). The big picture is, if we associate our impure hearts with pure love, (being corrupt)we then come up with a mess of ideas that have nothing to do with how God may be trying to get us to understand things. We ultimately reap the fruits that we sow. God says if we love mother father or child more than Him than we are not worthy of Him. Abraham even sacrificed his own child to God as a reference to something we must all do in terms of releasing our hearts to the one and only! The heart is the source of your focus and energy so if some person has that, naturally they will be tempted to manipulate or neglect it. Even the nicest of person. No man/woman can handle a heart in the way Jesus does. Now we can Entrust things to people but we cannot fully trust people with our own heart. Sometimes, you have put too much time and energy into a person or thing because you want to reap the benefits of that thing. But God tells us in many forms to render our hearts to Him. If we fully draw our hearts to others, then we will eventually reap the consequences of drawing it away from God because our everything will be in them instead of God. We show our Godly values instilled in that person rather than in God. We start to want to do everything for that person, we sacrifice for that person, we may even want to be like that person because, unknowingly they become an idol in our hearts.

PROMISCUITY AND THE HEARTS GRATIFICATIONS.. (A DEEPER LOOK)

We can sell ourselves completely cheap when we simply thrive off of man pursued intellect alone, because there is a way to be challenged with the right motives and intellect. The thought of tampering into a higher power has always been known to give people a sense of control, making them feel superior like they know something that no one else knows. Phraroh in Egypt, was reluctant in allowing the Isrealites to be set free, keeping them in bondage for power and control. Also, Phraroh's "wisemen" manipulated what is good by using the works of God to their own fleshly advantage. We know all works come from God. Making themselves as false "gods" by using magic/ powers obtained by the enemy, they go against the natural Works of God for the right uses, which is called witchcraft as is any kind of manipulation of the mind for personal pursuit or gain. We really don't have complete understanding to the depth of our Infinite source; So when we try, God empowers us to a certain extent. When we follow Him, knowing that He is God, we can rest assure that our Father won't keep any good thing from us. To use control for pleasure or gain makes a person feel powerful, but it cheapens there beauty that was originally given by God, let alone their character. They don't know where that source of energy comes from, they don't realize that it can and will make them feel empty and over stimulated to keep needing more. We all depend on a higher source. That is why intelligence has increased so much. If a person thinks they can learn their way to become as good as God, so did satan, and that person is being decieved by the source of energy that won't lead them to Heaven but instead in the opposite direction. Although all power comes from God, we know that certain powers are corrupted by the enemy and they aren't fit for God's Kingdom. Mankind wasn't made to burn for eternity, but through corruption we became seperated from God; He has nothing to do with the flesh. Flesh and blood will not inherit the Kingdom. When someone is using their intellectual skills for the wrong reasons it will leave them spiritually depraved. Even though we think we want what is tangible to a carnal nature, Our Spiritual nature wants what is higher; not only high, but pure; things that we can't obtain from the flesh. That's why there are people who only want a form of godliness, but deny the power of God by using there own methods. They are simply satisfied with intellectual relationships without actually seeking after, or talking about God. They expound on acedemics, sports, science, casual relations, they even relate to society, history and the list goes on. There is a big playground out there of things to come up with, of things to talk about and ways to do it through the flesh so you will never be bored; We are all Blessed but, their Blessings can be cheapened when they are taking bits and peices of the truth and steming their own method of thinking to manipulate, play, and control others, and have their way on this earth, while placing a title "Grown up" talk on things that deal with what God freely gives. Whew! We are not here to use these things for our own personal gain but to love God and love one another purely. We can't simply thrive off of intellect alone. It cheapens and discredits God for who a person really is. What about humility? If you take a peice of something away, sometimes it can instantly take away it's original form, and other times it will only keep changing until it completely takes away the form, so once you keep adding and taking away, you keep diluting and if you dilute the main source of what holds it all together, then it eventually leaves you with nothing. Humility is not how we appear to others, but how we develop TRUE concrete character through integrity from God. Not self-made, but self- diminished and CHRIST-centered.

(SCRIPTURE 2 Corinthians 3:18) "But we all, with open face beholding as in a glass the glory of the Lord are changed into the same image from glory to glory, even as by the Spirit of The Lord."

(SCRIPTURE1 John 3:2) "Beloved, now are we the sons of God, and it doth not yet appear what we shall be: but we know that, when He shall appear we shall be like Him for we shall see Him as He is."

When He shall appear, we shall be like Him! Some people now and days, Arouse emotions and feelings to get something out of the person in having the wrong motives. They don't labor to do it either, It's called witchcraft.

Being exposed to the spiritual things of God but using them in a carnal fashion for a carnal pursuit, is then become witchraft. Our human intellect is bad when we base it on carnal things or play with it in a carnal mindset, because we should always be reaching for something higher than our own pursuits. Some people reach a certain level of understanding that will gratify their fleshly nature and they find pleasure in maintaining just that. All sorts of rivers flow from what was built up by their own understanding of spiritual things. That means they are seeking spiritual things through a fleshly/ carnal mindset. So yes, we get enlightenment but remember satan was once an angel in Heaven too and has power to decieve. We only satisfy those deep things when we actually get to know the Creator of All things; hanging on tight to His truth and His Word. He wants us to understand that we can have an intellectual relationship with Him in getting to know Him. The time I spend with The Lord is the best time. I don't get misjuged or misguided. I get to feel His peace and yearn for His presence I get to work on focus to see His presence and He gives me new Revelations and mercies. He shows me what areas I need improvement, and He is always faithful even when lacking trust in Him. He brought us to His Word, and we realize that He brought us to the understanding as well through His Holy Spirit. Intellect is nothing, carnality is nothing, but the loving of and praising God is beneficial for all things! Everybody wants to be like Jesus but nobody wants to die to self. The secrets of life pertain to more than stimulating emotions, emotions are okay but when we learn to enjoy the bad ones while relying on a sober source, He wraps His arms around us with Blessings, peace and truth. God is a God of giving & we only try to catch up to Him, but we know All things through CHRIST. He is our leader and our prayers come to pass when we believe in Him for all things and trust that He is faithful. If it happens differently it's because He wants to make it come to pass more abundantly.

And God began again teaching us to want for nothing just like in the days of Numbers, when once the Isrealites were delivered out of the hands of the Egyptians they were being taught God's quality principles for heart guarding. He still teaches us this today. Want for nothing. If a man wants everything knowing it isn't good or beneficial in this life, how can it last? But that man will take it and run with it without considering that it's temporary. Well, God taught the Israelites by feeding them only bread in the wilderness, while they were complaining, God was teaching them principles that would keep them qualified to inherit the promiseland, having everlasting treasures. We all like them, have gone astray.

(SCRIPTURE Numbers 11:6 KJV) "But now our soul is dried away: there is nothing at all, beside this man'na before our eyes".

They began to remember the fleshly things that the Egyptians gave them in comparison to what they only saw at a glance. God was also teaching them patience. If not for that teaching, could they have been at the promisedland as soon as they crossed the waters? I don't know, but God taught them patience. Our whole being tends to get weary when we do things of the Spirit for a long period of time. But it's not a bad thing, because God wants to stretch us to our full potential even through being in the flesh. Too much of anything is not good, but when you have too much of the wrong things it's even worse. For example, T.V. Most things shown on television now and days are poisonous. So when you have poison floating through your mind on a daily basis or even most times, how are you going to hear the voice of God? It takes away truth and leads to compromise. A little bite of the apple goes a long way. I don't say this to scare you, I say it because it is true and if we really set out to do something, God will help us along the way. He is a generous God and freely gives us all things if we ask Him. There are no limits to obtaining the things we want and need with God.

There are no limits. There are situations where we can't help our circumstances and God is right there to understand each one of our needs. He wants to develop us and give us what we need in His fashion and way. As we develop and run His race, (not the race of the world; see that's a different race;) He assures us that we will obtain our Salvation. Inquiring minds like to be stretched in the things of God! *Our very own heartbeats yearn to develop the Character of, and things of God.* Each day as He shows us these things in His Mercy. Even those that don't walk in Him are granted the freedom to exercise His Glory. Unfortunately some people do it and use it for their shame. the term referred to as secularism. That just means anything Unholy. See God is a Holy God and He expects us to be like Him when it's all said and done. He is the one who already made the path, we just walk in it. God does not say to "follow your heart" He says to Love. If you follow your heart all the time, you may be going this place and that place, drinking whatever you want, eating whatever you want, etc; and you may be at the wrong places at the wrong time. You see, it's only when we realize who and what we are when we can understand that life isn't limited to this flesh and our carnal desires. The wind blows and we can't see it, In the same way the Spirit gives life in us and we cannot see it, Tho without Him, we are dead just like that. The life of a man is ordered, the death of a man is ordered and so is the heart of a man, to serve God! And God alone do we Worship; But when you give that precious heart to someone or something else, it is then considered an idol! God didn't create our heart to be promiscuous, He said to love Him with our whole heart whole mind and soul. Only then can we love others. We need a new heart and mind and to be renewed by a right spirit because the Spirit of a man is at war with the things and operation of God. We need to seek the heart of God and the only way to do that is by seeking Jesus and asking Him with faith! If you don't have faith, then ask Him for it! If you give your heart to a person, you begin to see how they see because they are what you start to idolize and follow. See the corruption of man is what sets us apart from God through disobedience; but we can be reconciled back to Him through faith which is the first step in our Salvation process. Our works are His works once we recieve

His baptism of The Holy Spirit, because only then is He able to create this pure heart and mind in us to renew us.

SCRIPTURE John 3:5 KJV "Jesus answered, Verily, verily, I say unto thee, Except a man be born of water and of the Spirit, he cannot enter into the kingdom of God."

So pray to recieve the Baptism of The Holy Spirit! We have to understand how God works. Again, Jesus comes to us through seeking Him with our whole hearts. Just as this world has a process, He has HIS own, and we start to see the Kingdom when we seek God!

I've learned that sometimes, just 1 bad choice leads to hundreds of other bad choices. We tend to take our mind off of what is good and feed the flesh when we make a bad choice because naturally, our mind starts to try and to develop a habbit.. A bad habbit is a pattern in your carnal nature, that is against your Spiritual nature in which the devil tries to use to control you. That's what I mean. he uses it to get you to do what is wrong. There is a time and a season for everything underneath the Heavens. There is a time for war and a time for peace excalimed in (Ecc 3:8 KJV)

This time we have left here is A great call for the lost sheep (God's people). It is the time to renew our God driven purpose of getting people to know The Lord and understand their purpose in life. It is a time for God to turn their hearts away from sinful practices; and that work can be complete when we personally submit to the calling of God in our lives. All of the beautiful things we see here point us back to our maker. We don't want to hear, "I never knew you". To know God is to spend time with Him. We can't make Jesus out to what we want Him to be (as they try and do so much now and days), nor can people bring Him to nought. But hollywood tries so hard to either understand, mock or imitate Our Creator. Sometimes I don't know which one and don't bother to care. I know that they have strayed away from the truth and have lost their minds for the wrong reasons. As stated before, people think there needs to be a work done, that's why hollywood tries to catch up to God in the wrong way; but God says the work is already complete and we just have to follow it. Who are we to judge anyone elses life? Even if it doesn't fit our own standards? For it is God that placed that person here, not man! His Holy Spirit is engrafted in each and every one of us when we cry out to Him and ask Him with our whole hearts. It's just that most times we don't take the initiative to ask Him for the things we need. We depend solely on ourselves and trust in our own minds for the things we need and are attainable to us, but we are precious in His sight. Anyone who tries to do the work of God becomes a target for satan but you have to complete the work set out for you, in knowing that you not only do these things in assurance to that you will spend eternal life with Him in Heaven, but that you represent a Holy and Just God so your works are not in vain! The fruit of your labor will be plentiful and you will hear the words "Well done thou good and faithful servant."

God is doing a distinct seperation between the wheat and the tares. He came to show us that He his the Word. and the letter is in our hearts so we must abide in His word knowing that the Word has no limit. The Holy Spirit is the one who helped us understand the Word. There are many people who are trying to understand the Word of God, and they can't. They say that it's old but, in seeing, they cannot percieve and hearing they cannot understand lest at anytime they shall Repent and God will take the veil from their eyes. So remember, the Word is alive and it is written down for our adminition. We are living The Word itself. Jesus came and showed them, He is the Living Word and is alive today! He will take us where we need to go, throughout His Word when our lives are submitted; And if they take the physical Holy Word from us, we'll still have it with us!

SCRIPTURE Luke 9:3 KJV "And He said unto them, take nothing for your journey. neither staves, nor scrip, neither bread neither money; neither have two coats apiece."; and then later in SCRIPUTRE, Luke 12:12 KJV "For the Holy Ghost shall teach you in the same hour what ye ought to say."

His Word is alive in His Holy Spirit through us!

Our whole life is about trusting God And getting to know Him. But some people don't realize it and have gone out of their way to justify sin. They have left the path of God to their own hurt. They don't realize that everything stems from God. That is what the tests we have, prove. They prove our trust in Him and reveal how much we had in the first place.

SCRIPTURE (Luke 12:42) "And The Lord said, who then is that faithful and wise steward, whom his Lord shall make ruler over His household, to give them their portion of meat in due season?"

It's about a relationship with our Creator, we must learn to trust Him.. Even if were taking step by step baby steps of faith He will walk with us! He entrusts us with His Word for us to choose to do the right thing, once we know truth. Even when people misuse The Word or put it out of context, The Lord still entrusts those who will walk firmly in it. Because we can walk firmly in it. It's just that sometimes we forget we have the choice. If our drive is based on our self-motivation, then we will be driven by our selves for ourselves, which drives us crazy! But when we get driven from true motivation towards God and getting to know Him, then we are driven by the right force. He is our only source it's just that not everyone realizes it. How much time do you spend getting to know God? Do you work most of your time to get money to pay the bills? Well honestly all that is going to be put to rest very soon. Even the very foundation we stand on, know and have gotten so comfortable with will be melted by flames of fire soon. Our attitude towards sin is always aggresive because of knowing and loving Christ. Our attitude towards God is always trying to get to know Him more and He keeps us learning more and more each day until we come unto the fullness Of Christ. We were made to serve and Love Him! We are ALL working to that point of limitless driven motivation for Him & that way, God gets to intervene on our behalf in places that we lack. He makes up for any lack when were following Him.

If people think there needs to be a work done, the end result will always lead to sacrifice and war. That is how satan captivates the minds of those who don't know the work is already complete. God already has a plan to save mankind from destruction, and a plan for evildoers. Why are people looking for peace on earth when God clearly tells us of our corrupt nature. Our peace comes through knowing Him, A man-made form of peace in which has no benefit to the afterlife will evaporate. If we think that something needs to be done about mankind don't we know that God knows that too? He says "I will not leave you comfortless" in (John 14:18 KJV)

One of the biggest deceptions that have stuck within our times is "What you don't know won't hurt you". It's funny because that is the exact opposite of what God says which is SCRIPTURE Hosea 4:6 KJV "My people are destroyed for a lack of knowledge: because thou hast rejected knowledge, I will also reject thee: that thou shall be no priest to me; seeing that thou hast forgotten the law of thy God, I will also forget thy children".

Now we have considered it to mean knowledge of this world, but what God really means is knowledge of Him and getting to know Him, that's all really. Loving, and spending time with Him. I've gotten to see how far away from God people really are and how much digging we need to do to get back to Him. Well, not really digging but, how He sometimes needs to reconstruct us back to nature when we subconsciously steer so far away from Him.

God is not the author of confusion so it is only when we seperate ourselves from Him that it becomes hard to hear His voice tho He's really not far away. He's got the Angels watching over us protecting us even tho we may not be able to see them. And He is coming for us like a theif. Just like Adam and eve were in the garden being watched He is watching our every move, motive and thought to see what we are going to do. Waiting for us to turn our heads this way and look straight up at Him. Because He is our God, our Father. For He says "Be still and know that I am God."

The enemy has people too stuck on themselves. God tells us that we have to fight our 3 oppressors, Our flesh, the enemy and the things of this world. In the endtime, lawlessness has abounded in many ways already as we can see through the news and many other sources. People don't care anymore. They've abandoned mercy, and life has been about achievements and success. So where are the ones in the Kingdom who will stand up for the truth? The whole time things have been designed to try and get your attention off of the tasks that God actually may be requiring you to do. Well through resistance, makes it harder and harder to push through to do the things of God. The same things that were designed for you, have become a "hinderance" for you to do, due to the obligations of society that we have sadly placed before God. Well, if we do have that blockage in our lives, God gives us the option of exchange. For what God might be trying to get us to do is far better than what we try to do for ourselves. That's just the truth, but when we come out of deciet, a lot of load gets lifted. People don't fully understand what is happening to you and that is why they may not like it. Never stop climbing to reach to The Heart of God. When we have an understanding of how He speaks to us personally, we are able to do the right things in life. Pray for understanding and wisdom and it is written to humble ourselves under the Mighty hand of God, and He will exhalt us in due time! He is faithful and will do as He promises! And we know that He gives us His mighty power and authority through the work of His Holy Spirit. The devil is playing people for a fool, and making them think that this life is the only one worth living, making them feel choked from spreading the love of God. But God made things simple for us. We don't have to go getting accustomed to the pattern of this world. It is only because of our lusts for other things that we hold onto anything that is given to us freely by God. God wants us to see that we can begin to break through our own foundation when we simply abide in the place that He's placed us. When we don't move out, we can remain in the vine and true source that everything else stems from.

Loving the unloveable

Even though our hearts are unloveable and desperately wicked, God still loves us. Only God can do that, we can't.

When we try, we end up giving them our carnal heart and mind.

(1 John 5:2 KJV) "By this we know that we love the children of God, when we love God, and keep His commandments"

God regenerates a pure heart in us each day when we give ours to Him.

(2 Timothy 2:22 KJV) "Flee also youthful lusts: but follow righteousness, faith, charity, peace with them that call on The Lord out of a pure heart."

Out of a pure heart tells us that we have to have a pure heart to even do this, but it shows us how the heart is desperately wicked SCRIPTURE (Jeremiah 17:9 KJV) "The heart is decietful above all things, and desperately wicked: who can know it?."

So if our heart is desperately wicked, then whose heart is pure for us to call out to? His heart and mind is our reassurace of a pure heart and mind. Our form of love that we grew up with through our carnal nature before fully coming to the understanding of God were through the works of the flesh ... ex: sinning/ or carnal love. there are different types of love we show & learn to share with others once we come to the knowledge of what it really means to love. God shows us that youthful lusts are contrary to sound love through SCRIPTURE (2 Timothy KJV) above. Works of the flesh and sin, means you hate a persons soul in the end, because the flesh can profit us nothing.

SCRIPTURE (John 6:63 KJV) "It is the Spirit that quickeneth; the flesh profiteth nothing: the words that I speak unto you, they are Spirit, and they are life."

Some people go out of their way to show thier form of love, even religous people. It is a form of love with no substance and no spiritual pruning or growth. It is vague and it gives birth to the flesh when it is operated from a fleshly motive, making people feel like they did something when we can do nothing. Our love is true genuine righteous and pure through the work of God that is already in existence before we came about! NO FLESH OR BLOOD WILL INHERIT THE KINGDOM OF GOD, we put a dent in our relationship with God through lack of trust and disobedience. Since we know that our flesh has to be destroyed and our temple is being used for Heavenly things, we know that we can't truly be saved by any work of our flesh, because that work has already been done through JESUS! Our carnal man will always be at enmity against God and this is why we must must put on Christ through the Holy Spirit. People believe love when they see it or feel it. God makes our love accountable when we do it.

SCRIPTURE KJV (1John 4:18 KJV) "There is no fear in love but perfect love casts out fear."

HOW TO LOVE PEOPLE

When God places a person in your life and you are unsure of them, it's usually because of what we see or how we feel that makes us unsure. I said, when GOD places that person in there. Our unsurety is usually our fear. We are lacking trust in the provision of God. He will tell you the answer once you wait on Him. Pray about them ... Pray once, twice, three times and it continues until you get a full grown understanding of the people God places in your life. No fear will interact with our love for The Lord, or His people. Amen. How do we show love the right way? Well, let's say you want to remodel your kitchen, and all you have is enough money to remodel half of the kitchen. The other half is for you to save for something else. Well, the person that wants to remodel your kitchen decides to give you mercy and cut your price down to what you can afford. So now, you have the price you can afford. So you give thanks to that person. Let's say the same person that gave you the cut from your bill, he on the same day went out and cursed and attacked someone. Well that is how our love is partial; but God makes our love accounted worthy. It is the Spirit of God that qualifies ones "good act." Only He can show us how to love the right way. He says "I will pour out of my Spirit upon all flesh"

(Acts 2:17 KJV) God made all of us in His image.

(Genesis 1:26 KJV) We have a carnal nature and a spiritual nature. Our Spiritual nature want the things of God, but our carnal nature was born for wrath and completely goes against God; the things we know by the flesh don't suffice us spiritually. And we know by what we do, contrary to the things of God that we do need cleansing, but our purification can only come from Him, so our efforts of love are still inadequate compared to a Mighty God. When Adam and Eve were in the garden (before they took on corruption in the carnal nature), that carnal nature was acceptable with God because it was purified by Him; but now, God tells us how flesh and blood will not inherit the Kingdom. God makes things simple for us. He expects us to read between the lines and use the sources that He's given us. If you have learned it from the Word of God, then it is true. It's up to us now to apply what we've learned and produce from it; and not only that, but to get good understanding of it. The flesh by nature, finds ways to make leisure of the things pertaining to our God. Sometimes satan has a way of making other things seem more important, so when it's time for the things of God, we rest on it. God assures us of a rest that He has for us. A rest that no man can give but only Him.

Our rest can be advantageous to us when we fully submit to the work created for us rather than the work we create for ourselves. We always have our own choices in life. Sometimes we go by what we witness, see, hear and experience in life which construct our way of thinking and our operation in life. While the world teaches us how to cope with physical/ carnal matters pertaining to this life, God teaches us more than how to just cope with, but how effectively deal with our carnal nature until we can kill these problems that stem from this nature. You may hear people tell you that it's natural to have sex, well yes, it is a union between Man and woman that comes from God and not man. He also gave us a spiritual nature to dictate the things that are an abomination unto Him so that we don't just solely rely on a carnal perspective. So when we submit even these things to God, we get full assurance of the right way to handle our carnal nature. See, our carnal nature is a problem with God (Romans 8:7 KJV) tells us. Not only is the carnal mind at enmity against Him but also our carnal bodies, it is written in (1 Corinthians 15:50 KJV) that flesh and blood cannot inherit the Kingdom. Our carnal nature is detestable to God; (Romans 8:8 KJV).

When we don't give in to the natural ways of man, God becomes natural to us and we can then see His way of seeing things. We can see His operation. It's not about being religous or knowing The Bible left to right. We are living the Bible even now and do some of the things we don't even know through our Spiritual nature. When we spend time with our creator He does things naturally through the Spirit in which we might not even be aware of. But others can see when we can submit all things to Him we get good foundational understanding.

THE CHURCH'S PROBLEM

As time changes and changes, demands increase due to our "trying to catch up to God". Our efforts get so drastic and when we try to do for ourselves, it can sometimes get in the way of God's ideal plan for us. When we try and think for ourselves, we come up with addition and subtraction and sometimes division, Even when we listen to the voices of others it can hinder us. Over the years, we have missed out on that time just being alone with God and praising Him remembering the places He's brought us from and where He's taking us. I'm not talking about a few hours out of the day, but more as making it our over powering lifestyle. And I don't mean us physically traveling to reap that experience, but through lifes everyday motions we need that time to step away from the crowd and society and just travel back with God, as a child. Most of our time spent with our creator benefits us the most with Him, and in life in general. God says to fear no evil. Some of the church's problem is fear. With true believers, it is the fear of God, and unwillingness to compromise. By all means, fear God! But trust the power that is in you to work behind you and before you while you are doing His work. Or are we fully surrendering our lifestyles to do His work? We still see The Holy Spirit at work today through the midst of this storm of life. Doesn't He answer our prayers? But God doesn't want to limit our exposure, He wants us to know that He is with us in all things and that He made all things. Not to be motivated to defend the things we fear by reacting to them through the flesh, or to be sufficed in the things we did & thought right, to prove the enemy's schemes. But to truly know what is right and exactly how to conduct ourselves through following the footsteps of The Only One capable of taking the keys of hell and death. We can overcome fear of the enemy, his agenda and schemes, and begin to love even our fellow decievers, when we truly understand who God is. Sometimes people in the Body of Christ may look like they have a wrong motive or are doing it all wrong and they are actually doing the work of God. They may have humbly submitted themselves to God. Let's take a rapper for example; traditional church goers may have a different opinion. Let's see if Jesus Himself solely bases His purpose on scripture alone but if He doesn't demonstrate to us through the Spirit and somewhere along the lines of scripture, that whatever He is doing, is in there. When Jesus and His disciples went to pluck the ears of the corn on the Sabbath. When Jesus healed on the Sabbath which was a "work" in the pharisees eyes. When Jesus told Peter in a vision to eat something that the old testament tells us is uncommon or unclean. When He justified the woman that was caught in the very act of adultery and told her not to sin anymore. If we live by the letter, we must keep the whole law! It says in (2 Corinthians 3:6 KJV)

"Who also hath made us able ministers of the new testament; not of the letter, but of the Spirit; for the letter killeth but the Spirit giveth life."

(James 2:10 KJV) says "For whosoever shall keep the whole law, and yet offend in one point, he is guilty of all." We know we are the children of God and that we are following Him. This is not a new doctrine. We have to trust that GOD IS REAL and Real in Us! And even though we might have a high calling in God, it is still Him! Think of Moses and how he betimes got humbled by The Almighty, yet God used him to part the seas! The life we live in, is part of the letter. We are the written epistles not made with ink!

(2 Co:33 KJV) "Forasmuch as ye are manifestly declared to be the epistle of Christ ministered by us, written not with ink, but with the Spirit of the living God; not in tables of stone, but in fleshly tables of the heart" We being evil, all of us through our carnal nature, are supposed to conduct ourselves in the way of Christ through mercy even in the confusing times, we follow what He did. Since we only know in part. I think that it's easy to attest to the fact that we only know in part. When Jesus comes, we will know more mysteries and they will be revealed.

(1 Co 4:5 KJV) "Therefore judge nothing before the time, until the Lord come, who both will bring to light the hidden things of darkness and will make manifest the counsels of the hearts: and then shall every man have praise of God". The pharisees lacked mercy because of fear, pride, and not wanting to trust God because of their own self-righteousness. So they missed out on the Glory of God through Our Lord and Savior Jesus Christ, and only got to see and experience freedom in Him, once they repented. Our fear comes by a form of self-righteousness and pride which alot of the church has today. Many are caught on themselves and the plan that God called them to do. But the problem is they are simply stuck on that. Yes we are to hold fast on the things we have learned by God, but God doesn't promote fear He promotes caution. God helped me realize, we must be elevated because the transformation begins, even when we recieve the gift of The Holy Spirit!

(1 Co. 15:58 KJV) "Therefore, my beloved brethren, be ye steadfast, unmoveable, always abounding in the work of The Lord, forasmuch as ye know that your labor is not in vain in The

Lord." Our work has to abound, and we must elevate with Our Savior! I'm not talking about "elevate yourself". This elevation comes only through the work of The Holy Ghost, and He will elevate you. We don't have to be fearful because we are free to explore and learn more and pretend like we don't even see any darkness. We are free to be like Jesus! He is our leader guider Commander and protector, and His command for us is to Follow Him! When we travel with Him, we then get to experience His walk and understand His truth better. We understand that we don't rely on ourselves as much as we think we do.. The church's conclusion is that we are in Revelation, YES! But it doesn't stop there. God says (Malachi 3:6 KJV) "For I am The Lord, I change not". (Hebrews 13:8 KJV)

"Jesus Christ the same yesterday, and to day, and for ever". This means, He will still proceed in the same promises that He's promised for us no matter the times we are in. He promised us that He goes before us and there is no need to fear (Deu 31:8 KJV) "And The LORD, He it is that doth go before thee: He will be with thee, He will not fail thee, neither forsake thee: Fear not, neither be dismayed."

(Matthew 28:20 KJV) "and lo, I am with you alway, even unto the end of the world. Amen." The outrage and chaos of society today only pressures us to be more preserved in prayer and ready to meet our Savior face to face. We don't have to worry much about the decievers because now it is for the most part too hard to tell. We must be willing to bear our cross and fight the enemys schemes. And we can look at how Jesus fought and Win! But when we fight those who proclaim Christ but may not fit into our understanding of what that person is supposed to look like proclaiming our Savior, we immediately doubt and fight against to try and prove them wrong sometimes hindering their growth in not knowing where they come from. (the levels of darkness are deep). We then defame and slander them in our own carnal way. It can push us back and others because we really don't know the reason why the person is that way. Even if we think were right, (take heed that we stand) The Bible says In (Proverbs 21:2 KJV) that "Every way of man is right in his own eyes". Do we take the time to think, "What if I was wrong about that person" Instead of being justified by the letter, (For God says if we keep the law then we must keep the whole law) and only Jesus can do that through The Holy Spirit in us today until He returns. We have to realize the devil tries to work in us through our flesh physically and through the flesh of the mind. Paul even said in (Romans 7:14 KJV) "For we know that the law is spiritual: but I am carnal, sold under sin. For that which I do I allow not: for what I would, that do I not; but what I hate, that do I. If then I do that which I would not, I consent unto the law that it is good. Now then it is no more I that do it, but sin that dwelleth in me. For I know that in me (that is, in my flesh,) dwelleth no good thing: for to will is present with me; but how to perform that which is good I find not. For the good that I would I do not: but the evil which I would not, that I do. Now if I do that I would not, it is no more I that do it, but sin that dwelleth in me. I find then a law, that, when I would do good, evil is present with me. For I delight in the law of God after the inward man: But I see another law in my members, warring against the law of my mind, and bringing me into captivity to the law of sin which is in my members. O wretched man that I am! who shall deliver me from the body of this death? I thank God through Jesus Christ our Lord. So then with the mind I myself serve the law of God; but with the flesh the law of sin." So sometimes we skip on making sure through asking in prayer but everything looks wrong and there is tons of confusion in the world now so we instantly judge by appearance of how things look. See (John 7:24 KJV)

We have to come out of ourselves and lay ourselves completely down, everyday. And not defame our bretheren. Due to lack of understanding. Remember, we are learning new everyday. We don't believe our prayers because of what we did, but because of what Christ did for us. And He doesn't answer us according to what we do, but by His mercy.

"Be still and know that I am God"

(Psalm 46:10 KJV) Not only is it in dancing where we question a persons motives, referencing a particular way they might dance. But even in the way they speak Or look. satan plays unfair and once we realize the things that are sin, vs the things a person may or may not be able to control, then we can move along faster with achieving the goal that God has for all of us to attain. It's in the way a person looks, walks, talks, and yes, even dresses that may be a part of what they cannot control. Now God says "You will know a tree by it's fruit." in (Matthew 7:16 KJV)

But in other versions they say different things.. Also, God also tells us to rightly judge. People come from every different background and culture, different ways of understanding to different preferences. We have to know what sin is so the devil won't confuse us. Growing up, some people were taught not to wear certain clothes or not to look a certain way, act or even dance when going to church because we were taught these things were inappropriate for church. I've learned overtime that some of the things I do personally are not innapropriate and my mind will be in Heavenly places, it is just pare of the nature of how I dance or walk. You may think that I am trying to walk with a switch but you have no idea that my leg and back has been hurting all day for example. Throughout time, the church has forgotten what it means to be Holy and replaced Holiness with a set of rules and regulations or made it seperate from what we are even able to apply in our daily lives as believers. God tells us to be Holy even as He is Holy so in order to do that it's great to know how His Holiness is and how to apply it in us being human. Well, Holiness isn't a set of rules and regulations for us to follow, Holiness is seperation from sin and seperation from corruption. God also tells us how there is a time for everything under the Heavens. He tells us this through nature itself, let alone through our carnal nature. In these times, we understand that the things we see are getting more and more corrupt so God, in Revelation warns us to "Come out of her my people". That plead is for all mankind to come out of the corrupt system of this world as it grows more and more seperate from the natural ways of God. We learn that in anything we want to do or make better requires sacrifice, but just like read above, we can't sacrifice the foundation or quality things for things that aren't natural because it leaves us naked without Jesus! We weren't naturally set up for sin because it is damaging to our bodies, souls and mind. God has a plan to completely destroy sin at it's root. Anyone who wants to come out of sin must go to God first because only He can give us what we need to stop the corruption from taking over our being.

He is the one who made us and so He knows exactly those things we need to survive forever. Not like the term, "Forever young". We're talking about things that pertain to more than this world. What is a bad instrument? From what I know all instruments are considered good, the last time I checked. And if I dance a certain way, what does that say about me? Nothing because God made me to dance and in fact I'm even justified in the way I dance in (Psalm 149:3 KJV) it says to let them praise God dancing and singing with instruments and so ... Why should we be stopped from dancing because we don't dance like you? God gives us this freedom and also tells us that we are in Heavenly places. This earth is corrupt, and I don't want any part of the compromise I've been told to conform to. Sin starts in places that we can't see but it is so easy to point out the things that we do see. I also know that we are to rend our hearts and not our garments.

(Joel 2:13 KJV). Because our garments only constist of things that pertain to the flesh. Things that are in the flesh don't please Our Holy Father. Jesus told the pharisees how they make the outside of the cup clean but can't make the inside clean. They consistently look well to everybody but how come they can't effectively change their hearts. They would critcize you for dancing for example or judge you by how you, or it looks; Yet why do they keep on sinning and aren't able to stop and then go back and point to those people just like them? They didn't want to accept Jesus, and they were stuck in sin. Well it is the same way in some churches today, we have to know what sin is, and know what it means to be Holy or else we walk around thinking that were something were not.

When we get to Heaven it says in Matthew 22:12 "And He saith unto Him, friend how camest thou in hither not having a wedding garment? And he was speechless". Well not only that, that unprofitable servant was cast out for not having on a wedding garment! Well what is the garment since Jesus clearly teaches us that we can't be righteous on the outside. And how do we know what to wear to be accepted by Jesus?

(2 Corinthians 4: 4 KJV) "In whom the god of this world hath blinded the minds of them which believe not, lest th light of the glorious gospel fo Christ, who is the image of God, should shine unto them". One of the best things is to know that we have full

access to the knowledge of our God and Savior and even though in this world, the truth seems to get diluted; that just isn't possible. Some of the secrets that have been found out by man are not new discoveries to God, but were made tangible to us from the beginning, and they point us right back to the beginning. Those discoveries are not to be made idols or to be made into anything we set our hearts on, and they are sometimes used in the wrong way. But when applied in the right way, does God have a problem with that? Well, I can say that God has always had a problem with sin! He never from the beginning had a problem with man and carnality because He made us. And now, our choices are what Our Father is concerned with. He provides us with the understanding and it is up to us to give Him complete recognition and time. He gives us the access no matter where we are or what may or may not be around us for use, we still have much access to Him, and that is just so beautiful! We don't have to figure out everything on our own but God puts us in a place to love Him so much where we just want what He wants like what He likes and love what He loves. He doesn't tell us that we have to search high and below, He tells us to trust in Him. It's not hard to compromise in a world full of it. But it's harder to say yes to God and do right. The more you do right, the easier it becomes; the more you do wrong the less chance you desire to do right. Fear plays a big role into doing what's right, but God warns us that the fearful and non-believers shall all perish in the lake of fire (Rev. 21:8 KJV). All things are to be made to give Glory to God and that is our sole purpose anyway as believers to Give Him Glory!

HYPOCRITICAL CHARACTERS

(Luke 6:46 KJV) "And why call ye me, Lord, Lord, and do not the things which I say?" We have to know what The Lord says. Flowers need sunshine, rain and soil to be produced in the right way but all these things come by the one who supplies all. So when it starts to grow, it can become a bud, then it spreads until it eventually develops. It endures heat storms, wind, and cold and even sometimes snow through the changing seasons, but taken care of by the right owner, it still becomes a full grown flower. Like the changing seasons that God gives us by nature for for each year, He also gives us seasons to grow and develop in character. To know what The Lord says is to trust His Word. Everything is produced by faith, even this very earth that stands. "Through faith we understand that the worlds were framed by the word of God. so that things which are seen were not made of things which do appear."

(Heb 11:3 KJV) So in like manner, we also have to have understanding. "Knowing this that the trying of your faith worketh patience" (James 1:3 KJV)

So like the flower, we are tried and we start to see the sin in ourselves and areas that need pruning & to know what the Lord says and to grow, we have to have faith and patience. The voice of the Lord is seen in many different ways, even throughout nature, we can understand and learn to listen to His voice. But not just thorughout nature, it can even be in a quiet room alone, you can still hear His voice. Once we understand God's voice, we can learn to trust His leading for all things and carry out His plan effectively in our lives, neverminding the circumstances going on around us; the people either. People wont need to be our primary source of information, rather The Holy Spirit who teaches us all things. "But the Comforter, which is the Holy Ghost, whom the Father will send in my name, he shall teach you all things, and bring all things to your rememberance, whatsoever I have said unto you."

(John 14:26 KJV) "But the anointing which ye have recieved of Him abideth in you and ye need not that any man teach you". We have many preachers, evangelists, pastors and teachers, and these all are for exhortation and confirmation to the things God for us, but He teaches us naturally through The Holy Spirit. So in this time, there are many who do the works of God by their own greed and gain because they thrive off of the things given to them without fully submitting their hearts to the one who gave it them. We as the children of God submit to only one which is God, and we don't need to develop from confirmation of others, we need to develop by character potrayed by Him. We can have a tunnel vision in uncomfortable enviornments. We can still also be able to still concentrate on the things of God with the many divisions, churches, prophecies, and happenings around us and even the things people say that aren't true about us. We can experience the true love and power of God when we endure through all and stand still not worrying about what the devil is doing.

HOW TO HEAR FROM OUR GOD

What we spend our time doing is the essential part of our lives, because #1 it pleases God when we spend time with Him through faith, and 2, we get to reap the benefits of the time we spend getting to know Our Creator. That is two times the pleasure!

(Ecclesiastes 11:6 KJV) "In the morning sow thy seed, and in the evening withold not thine hand: for thou knowest not whether shall prosper, either this or that or whether shall prosper, either this or that, or whether they both shall be alike good."

Throughout the Word of God, the work that God has always called man to do was always His work for the Kingdom. Take a look at the Apostles, (when Jesus called them) they left their positions as fisherman or whatever it was they were doing, tax-collector etc. We can have in abundance, the seeds that we sow for ourselves and for others when we are constantly in a place where we can recieve seeds. Whew! I know that was a tounge twister; but Jesus uses the parable of The Sower in (Matthew 13 KJV) and there it mentions The Sower, (who is God), sows seeds among us.

(Matthew 13:3 KJV) "And He spake many things unto them in parables, saying, Behold, a sower went forth to sow; And when he sowed, some seeds fell by the way side, and the fowls came and devoured them up: Some fell upon stony places where they had not much earth: and forthwith they sprung up, because they had no deepness of earth: and when the sun was up they were scorched; and because they had no root, they withered away. And some fell among thorns; and the thorns sprung up and choked them, but other fell on good ground; and brought forth fruit, some an hundredfold some sixty fold some thirty fold. Who hath ears to hear, let him hear."

But in Galatians 6:8 He says "For the one who sows to his own flesh will from the flesh reap corruption, but the one who sows to the Spirit will from the Spirit reap eternal life". He shows us that we also have seeds that we sow among others by His Spirit. He wasn't just talking about physically tilling the land, but in a Spiritual sense as well. So we recieve our seeds to sow from Him! Whenever we are doing the work of God, it must be His work, not our own. Considering the times they were in, Jesus started to command the gentiles to repent. He no longer worked as a carpenter when He was ready to go out in the world to finish the works of God. Now is the time we are to finish The works of God as well through His Spirit. There comes a time in a person's life where, God will call them out. He says the laborurers are few". Why? cause they're out busy doing there own work. There is a time and a season for everything under the Heavens and He says we can discern the face of the sky but how come we can't discern the times we are in. We depend too much on other sources to tell us. We have the news and the media, tons of internet sources, even still, the Newspaper or magazines other people and churches! One of The most indirect ways to seperate ourselves from God and concrete truth is to rely on ear tickling preachers, and any other source that will feed our fleshly carnal nature. In fact that's a quick way to be going in the opposite direction away from God. Sometimes people don't want to admit we have it, but death is one proof of the nature of our corruption. It would insult God to think that He would limit us to the things of the flesh when this flesh cannot last forever. We can't count the things God is doing for us, when were spending our time with Him because though they are unseen, they are happening. So we must sow our seed next to our father, wherever we spend the most time growing is effective to what we will be sowing and how we will reap. Some people may go to church but still don't know The Father. That's because they never spent the time with Him. This generation likes to feel the rush, they treat eachother inhumane and have lack of true self-identity. But we learn our identity once we fully surrender our hearts to our Father. Only then will we not lack identity, we won't be idle, and we can sow and prosper from the fruits we bare.

(John 15:5 KJV) "I am the vine, ye are the branches: He that abideth in me and I in him, the same bringeth forth much fruit: for without me, ye can do nothing". God's voice is not a matter of when we want to hear it, it is a matter of when and how He decides to make Himself heard, because He knows how to reach our heart when we submit to Him by making ourself available. You ever wonder why people fall asleep while reading the Bible or hearing a sermon? Well because, Our Spirit man is being put to work. If there flesh is constantly at work, that means the Spirit man is dried up a little bit and may need a little extra oil. Either that or the sermon is boring. We need that oil to be completely full and ready with our lamps lit high waiting on our Savior, so we through the work of The Holy Spirit must drain the carnal man. If we constantly evacuate spending our time with God, and not meeting up with Him like the prophets of old, how can we truly say that we hear Him? In the churches through the preachers or Through every other curse word by the people we hear around us? Part of draining the carnal man is facing physical lonliness and a little discomfort at first. Cause a person who believes in God like he says he does knows they're never really alone. We just have to learn to trust in Him, and turn down the opinions of man.

"Neverthelesss I am continually with thee: thou hast holden me by my right hand." Psalm 73:23-24

But once you get to learn God's voice, you wouldn't have it any other way cause He listens too; and provides, protects just like He says He's gonna do. He doesn't judge or condemn you and honestly just wants to hear your problems. You start to see how natural it is to totally rely on and trust Him. Anything that you lack, He is affectionate towards your needs, and if at any point things seem different, that's because He's getting you to that place of complete reassurance. Keep your eyes on Him. He came for us to be healed and to remember that our suffering for this present time is not worthy to be compared to the Glory that will be revealed.

ADAM AND EVE WITH THE TEMPTER

When we get to know God, He not only shows us the real truth, but He rules out everyone else's ideas or opinions. Sometimes we get taught by phenominal leaders, about what happened to mankind's fall; And God has a way of showing us a deeper Revelation of those very things we know.

(Genesis 1:27 KJV) "So God created man in His own image, in the image of God created He Him; male and female created he them."

(1 John 3:2 KJV) "Beloved, now are we the sons of God, and it doth not yet appear what we shall be: but we know that, when He shall appear, we shall be like Him; for we shall see Him as He is."

(2 Corinthians 3:18 KJV) "We all, with unveiled faces, are looking as in a mirror at the glory of the Lord and are being transformed into the same image from glory to glory; even as by the Spirit of The Lord."

(Genesis 3:1-5 KJV) Marks the start of all temptation that is common to man. So now we know how we are made after the image of Jesus, The Son of God. Even from the beginning The Lord poured out His spirit on mankind, that's how we are able to do all of the things we do today. Since society has prospered so much in it's ways, it is inevitable that they will try to climb to the height of God. Well just like in the days of the tower of babble, man has seperated themselves from God by going about their own way to reach Him and find out His ways. Mankind wants to establish freedom from fleshly bondages and limits, by attaining authority from our own creator. All the while, God wants to be our Father and still reaches out His hand giving us a way to be saved from our own selves through repentance.

(John 10:1 KJV) "Verily, verily I say unto you, He that entereth not by the door into the sheepfold, but climbeth up some other way, the same is a thief and a robber." Jesus wants us to know how we get through His door is by Him; for no man can come to the Father but by Jesus! Throughout the Word we see how we can reach Him by listening and staying close to Him. "My sheep hear my voice, I know them, and they follow Me."

(John 10:27 KJV) He is Holy and we need to be Holy too, for He says "Be ye Holy, for I am Holy". To be Holy means to be seperated and distinct. Seperate from the sin of this world and that is what makes us a peculiar people. We are following after a Holy and Mighty God who has a Mighty purpose for each of our lives. His whole purpose for us here on earth (amongst many other things), is to save mankind from destruction caused by mankind. Also to give us an eternal home and resting place. Things have a way of seeming as though there not, and that is because of the deciever satan. Since the beginning, he has made things to seem as though they're not. Anything prosperous is not by anything that we do, but by the mercy of a Holy and Seperated God! He allows the enemy to prosper for a time, but then after that, Jesus fasted for 40 days and 40 nights and after that He was tempted by the devil in (Matthew 4:1-11 KJV). The first time, He was tempted by bread. The second time it was by pride. The last temptation was for the things of this world, for example: Money, clothes, Mansions, cars etc. as we see today. "Remember what I told you; 'A servant is not greater than his master.' If they persecuted me, they will persecute you also, If they obeyed my teaching, they will obey yours also." So if satan tempted Jesus with all these things, we too must be tempted by the things of the flesh but if we resist temptation then we are able to go in the works of God. The carnal man wasn't meant for hell. it was for satan and his demons. We took on that carnality once Eve listened to, and did something other than what God told her to. We take on that same nature and that is why we wrestle against spritual things in high places and try to fight to dumb ourselves down from the things we learn by the world. We truly are Spiritual beings in carnal bodies. These things we know, were meant for God to show us at His appointed time in His appointed way. The wisdom of this world is foolishness with God.

(1 Corinthians 1:21) "For after that in the wisdom of God the world by wisdom knew not God, it pleased God by the foolishness of preaching to save them that believe".

So because they have strayed so far away from God to try and become like gods themselves and have gotten so wise in their own eyes, brought on through corruption of Adam and Eve, the foolishness that we preach today pleases God. Not the things that go against Him or His Word. But the church is a mess and all over the place, and the condition can be cleaned up when our hearts and mind are directed in the right way towards Him, for He says ...

(1 Peter 3:21 KJV) "The like figure whereunto even baptism doth also now save us (not the putting away of the filth of the flesh, but the answer of a good conscience toward God) by the resurrection of Jesus Christ: So it's a matter of our Conscience towards Him.

"For if our heart condemn us, we know that God is greater than our heart and knoweth All things:

(1 John 3:20 KJV). Cause we know that our impure hearts are decietful (Jeremiah 17:9 KJV)

"The heart is deceitful above all things and desperately wicked: who can know it?"

The carnal mind and carnal heart has already been evaluated by Our specialist so all we need to do is come to the same conclusion that He tells us, which is to give it to Him where it belongs. And that is how we can come to a new way of thinking and understanding and perceiving things. Example Mary and Martha. Martha thought too much while Mary didn't think at all, she knew; and that's really what God wants us to do. Come out of our minds. We can enjoy the fruits of this life because we have to go through it. But Jesus left us example of how to pursue this life as pilgrims here on earth. He was without, and He sacrificed all so that we could be saved. Now that His Spirit is in us, we have to do the same for Him and our brothers and sisters in The Lord. We must come out of ourselves and into His Grace. Come out of our carnal way of thinking and mediocre way of percieving truth based on self-gratification. Sacrifice all in faith and use this world as not abusing it and He promises us He will give us much more!

(1 Corinthians 7:31 KJV) "And they that use this world, as not abusing it; for the fashion of this world passeth away".

That is how we come to the understanding that when God calls us out, it is for His divine purpose and plan not for something we thought to do by ourselves.

NEVER SATISFIED

Our flesh is never satisfied, but we always want things that never satisfy us. Things that only leave us hungry for more and dependant on more; but what about basic things we need to survive? In some cases, people (not just in other Countries), but in our very own Country, aren't able to attain food which are the basic things we need to survive, so said ... God is our supplier in all aspects of things. The things that we can't attain and the things that we can. Whether we eat physical food or Spiritual meat, we must put on Jesus Christ who is capable of all things; Our body is His temple so are we now capable? God is right there to fill the gaps in between the things we simply cannot attain, and things that we can attain. But as for the things that we attain by our own effort, sometimes it's easy to lose focus on who really made us capable of attaining it, when we feel as though we did the work.

Were always left with a choice. Our meat, (in these days) has to be the finished work of The Holy Spirit so that we can attain life. The Word is flying off of the pages into our hearts and although it can seem disguised through different, various versions, (not to mention the Word being banned in some cases, flagged and manipulated by false converts,) that doesn't cease the work of The Holy Spirit. If our conscious mind can recieve the things of God on good grounds, then He is ready to complete His work in us. He says that we must become as little children.

(Matthew 18:3 KJV) We know we are not limited to The physical Word alone because we are living it, it is active and alive through The Holy Spirit of Our Lord! There is nothing new under the sun, but God tells us that there is a new era and expansion of revelations in these last days. These are only new to us in the physical realm but they are written for us already, they are not new to God! We are living out the very Word that we see written down for us.

We are seeing the pages come to life and everybody has their own part or parts. This is why it is written that people will be searching to and fro looking for The Word as it was prophesied by Amos, "And they shall wander from sea to sea, and from north even to the east, they shall run to and fro to seek the word of the LORD, but they will not find it." Amos 8:12 The word has to be written in our hearts and sealed up. It is also written in Daniel 12:7 how Our Lord will have accomplished to scatter the power of The Holy people. His power is scattered from sea to sea. Why this is the very bread of life! Now, every single effort to diminish truth is being made, so we must attain His Word in our heart. We gravitate toward the temporary things because they are easier on our flesh but they make room for less improvement or growth when we suffice them. And when we feel like we have already put on so much resistance to our bodies, we seek rest.

Well, God tells us to give no provision for the flesh for a reason in Romans 13:14 "But put ye on The Lord Jesus Christ, and make not provision for the flesh, to fulfil the lusts thereof." But we are to rest in Him. He is our rest, and in due season He will provide the thing that we need. He must accomplish His works in us. While evil spirits wander to and fro seeking rest, our resistance to evil hits them & they have to find it in another place, but not you! cast them into the swine! The devil tries to feed you things of the flesh so often to make you dependent on things of the flesh, so we must crucify our flesh through the work of The Holy Spirit. It is attainable in different ways other than fasting, but fasting is a great way. Pray to The Lord to recieve His truth about resistance and He will show you!

MATURE LOVE AND HOW WE GET THRILLS THROUGH OUR ZEAL FOR GOD!

Being young, I used to like what is considered the wrong idea of maturity. So sometimes, I would limit myself to a simple demonstration of it in the way I would conduct myself; Until Eventually, I started to want to become mature in the things of God, once I began to know Him. He has shown me that His wisdom is truly out of this world (Seperated and peculiar). He shows me that He could have created the earth in one day but that He chose to do it in 7 because there is beauty in the process of nature. He shows me that the things we don't like, happen to us only to prune our minds, concrete our character and form our mature God-like being in HIM, for HIM." And the Lord said unto Moses, See, I have made thee a god to Pharaoh: and Aaron thy brother shall be thy prophet." Exodus 7:1 Now what God means is, the closer we come to Him, the more we begin to look like Him and show forth fruits of His maginificent Holy Spirit! Some things may hurt us through the process of pruning, but we get stimulated by the growth of getting to know God. We get the thrill of the chase for eternal instead of temporary. Have you ever felt your hair growing before? Or when someone gently massages your head it makes you wanna go to sleep? That's because when your head gets massaged, it helps it to grow through stimulation. When you think of a hair folicle, it gets stimulated by growth, the process deals with the (erector pili), muscle attaching below the gland to a fibrous layer around the outer sheath of the hair and the muscle has to contract and cause the hair to stand up and it also secretes oil. So even if it doesn't hurt your head for your hair to grow sometimes, the process of it actually coming out into a full grown hair takes work to bust through the follicle. We mature in the things of God and start to see His process in our lives through submission and obedience. We need to see and trust that The Lord is good, it is written "O taste and see that The Lord is good: blessed is the man that trusteth in Him" (Psalm 34:8 KJV).

By nature do we mature in God? Well, yes ofcourse we can if we allow time. Contrary to our spiritual nature, the carnal mindset doesn't want to submit to the things and nature of God. To love God is to learn to love His ways. Now my conduct will never be limited to the outside appearance of things because of what God did and is doing. How the world sees me and how I conduct myself doesn't matter to me anymore which makes me go full force into the things of God. And now your conduct doesn't have to be limited to the things of this world either, if that was your idea of maturity ;) Maturity is not only in being Kings or Queens of this world drinking wine, having your bills paid on time and fufilling worldly responsiblites that only limit and pertain to things of this life, because sometimes, we gotta give those things up. But now, we are capable of becoming mature in the things of God to experience His likeness and goodness.

When we grow spiritually, it is because we choose to exercise the Nature of The Son of God being lived out in us. Just how the nature of plants grow from the sun (The foundation of earth's energy and maintenence) Spiritually the same thing applies in us as well. We, by nature grow from being developed in the presence of the Son. We aren't just physical beings, so God made these physical things for us as Spiritual beings too/ our inner man. God is the Ultimate source of energy and if we don't apply our God given nature to praise Him, then we aren't giving even ourselves the benefits that we need, let alone Glorifying Our God who made us! In (1 John 2:6 KJV) It reads "He that saith he abideth in Him ought himself also to walk, even as He walked". So that we can abide in Him perfectly, we have to go back to the roots and see where everything stems from. I know sometimes in our walk we can be negligent and selfish towards the things of God so then we start to forget that it's from God that we have anything we have. But God is merciful and lets us know that we can go back to Him when we've done wrong, with faith and believing that we can, we can do all things. It can get hard to trust Him for things when we think were depending on ourselves, but God is faithful and knows all things. It is so easy to turn to the things were used to and trust the sources we are so reliant on in our everyday lives, they give us good information and tell us things we wanna hear and sometimes things we don't, but they give us ways of fixing problems that are common and relatable to our circumstances. The thing I notice about that though, is that the problems I get from them are only temporary and they make me dependent on them like the news and the media might give me my fix for the day but I feel like I gotta keep going back to them. That's because weve come up with ways of handling the problem without truly rooting it up or solving it but we place a bandaid on top of it and leave it at that. God wants to heal us from the things we don't like. We don't have to accept what we don't like about society or try to even change it ourselves. Yea we might be considered an outcast but so was the one who saved us. Not only that, as time goes on, peoples hearts start to change because God can change them. We do our part, He can do His, but He doesn't compromise with corruption not even for our sakes because He is a Holy God. He takes us step by step.

OUR COURTSHIP WITH GOD

Have you ever been married, or seen an engaged couple before they were about to get married? Well if you have, you may be familiar with the term "Courtship". It is a period of time for development between two to become one and unified. During that time two get to experience individual likes, intrests, different behaivors and traits about one another. Pastor asks this question, Will you have so and so to be your husband/wife; and you have to submit to that statement; Or in Court, where the judge will ask you, How do you plead? Well with God, we give our verbal form of consent which will be our testimony in Heaven. We go through our season of courtship with Jesus to become be-wedded that way when The Bridegroom comes, instead of Him considering us due to our circumstances or for any reason, He automatically accepts us to be His bridegroom once we have accepted Him and are ready to walk with Him through thick and thin, and we are ready to be His Bride. The Court system has their order and jurisdicitons, but God has His as well. Through our season of courtship we get over alot of problems that we have caused through sin. We get over the sinful nature and are pruned by God himself. Many people (even those that are close to us), don't understand what is happening to us through this season or why we act the way that we do, but it is our most intimate time we have with God. You see a new born baby teething and throwing a fit getting mad because they hurt and don't know what is happening to them? Or when you see the mother when she's about to give birth. Well so is being a true born-again Christian. I am proud to say that If you knew me about 16 years ago I was not the same person I am today because of the change that Jesus is bringing to completion. I didn't understand life at all and in fact, I was completely decieved by the enemy. I had no knowledge of what life is and what it means to be a christian because I had no structure, but I confessed Jesus as my Lord and Savior at an early age and I actually found Him at a later age. God took me the rest of the way! Alot of times, people lack trust in God because of His people; not understanding that we, (His people) will never add up to the amount of love that is in us. We only add up to a part of His love and that part is solely because of His Holy Spirit. He is our addition that we need to be any good thing we are or do any good thing that we do. We know in part and prophesy in part. Does that mean we can't obtain Holiness? Well, Not exactly since we have already obtained it, when were following Him. Our temples are the resting place of His Spirit when we follow His lead. His love is in each and every person on this planet and His Mercy too, Not just those who profess His name! It's only up to us to accept it and once we do, we are considered His children.

THE STORY OF NATALIE

There was this woman who was always nice and sympathetic. She always did the best she could and she kept her morals in tact most of the time to the best of her knowledge. She did not sin. She liked red rubies and diamonds, and those red rubies to match her favorite color lipstick, guess which one it was? Yep, red. She always thought that lipstick wouldn't make a woman a prostitute just like riding in a limosene doesn't make a person rich; She had the right attitude about life and she never had a problem with her advesaries but, they always seemed to have a problem with her. Now oneday she was walking to the store when there were 2 women passing by. She didn't mind them but kept on going to her destination until all of a sudden, her destination became short because she only got to go as far as 10 mins away from her house when these women started causing trouble. They set tacs on the ground as she passed them by, so she would step on them and fall. So she did. She stepped on the of he tacs in her way, fell on the ground with her feet bleeding and began crying and shouting due to the pain. And with her looking back (after they had passed her laughing,) and so she started cursing to the women as she was crying hurt and confused as to why they would do that. She was one to try her best to do right. She really just didn't understand the message of hate because all she did was love.

She even knew that in the Bible it says you reap what you sow so she was just confused because she felt like she clearly didn't do anything to reap that. Not too long after the cursing, the women came back her way and grabbed her by her hair and clothes, and all of her pretty red lipstick began to smudge on the concrete soon because they began smearing her makeup onto the ground. Those 2 women became the foundation for her new belief and morals of right and wrong behavior. The women left her there on the ground after they caused such an uproar against her life, and she was there to bleed and cry. She got up and decided to turn back around, go home & not continue her destination to the store but instead hide her face as she walked back on the way home to clean herself up. Her new moral standards now became," never go to the store alone being a woman; especially not in the dark or after a certain time period". She must have done alot of thinking on the way back home in between time but that was the execution plan for her idea of right and wrong behaivor even though it wasn't a commandment from God. Now, when the 2 girls got home, they decided that what they did was a good idea; and they had much to say about the woman on the way, who they tripped and hurt badly. They were talking and laughing about it so much that they began to actually inquire about other victims.

The girls were on the bed of one of their houses and they decided to order some pizza and watch movies while staying in the rest of the night; Then they called up some of their other friends to talk about what just happened and the pizza man rang the door bell. The pizza man was a nice looking gentleman so when one of the girls got up to get the door, she saw him and was a little perplexed and couldn't concentrate enough to get her money out correctly. She closed the door slightly and told him to hold on a minute as she raced sliding across the floor to go get her friend and tell her what she saw. Both of the girls came back to see the pizza man poking their chest out and twirling their hair and earrings, and he had a stunned look on his face so he asked them "How much will it cost me to fix the mess I made?" The girls stopped for a minute and wondered why he said that or if he was just trying to throw a pick up line at them. One of the girls answered (being promiscuous), "Well it's free, if you do for me a nice service". The service she wasn't talking about was delivering the pizza. So he just blushed a little and nodded "here's your change,." He said "Thank you", and as he walked away after being harrassed by the 2 women he was a little bit annoyed but not too long after being annoyed, he began to have other thoughts thinking, "hmmm.. I actually liked that", and he had a little bit more enthusiasm about the next house. The women came back in the house and got back on the phone to tell their friends about the pizza man and how he was so cute and all of the things that they wanted to do to him.

Until about 12am when they crashed and went to sleep. They got up the next day around 9 am and wanted to start the day fresh, hopefully with it being the same way it was yesterday. So they started scheming and plotting on what to do next and where they could cause trouble. One of the women (grown women), decided to tell her friend a secret about herself while they were coming up with these wicked ideas. She said "Ashley, I have a secret can you keep it?." And she responded "Why not". So she started to break down, crying about how her ex used to molest and hit her younger sister, and that when Ashley would always see them argue, not long after Ashley left the scene, her and her now (ex boyfriend) would physically fight and it always ended up with her going to the bar drinking so that's how she became a drunk. She started confessing many other things that she never got over while growing up. While Ashley was listening to her, she placed her head on her shoulder and the woman kept crying and crying, trying to explain to her that it wasn't her fault and that she felt the only way that she could keep him around was if she just allowed the situation to persist and hopefully he would stop abusing her little sister. Ashley replied,

"You should have told me this a long time ago", being as though they knew eachother for 10 years now. She said "It's okay, it's okay" as she kept her head rested on her shoulder. Once the girl got up, she went to go wash her face and Ashley didn't like the feeling she got with the things her friend told her.

Ashley started feeling sorry for her friend and she wasn't the "type" to feel sorry, and she wasn't the type to be nice to anybody unless she really liked them; and even though that was her friend, she couldn't shake the feeling. When she came back to Ashley, she found her twirling on her bed and saying weird stuff like "you can't make me, you can't make me" and "This isn't me, I'm good at nothing" wrestling back and forth on the bed with herself, so the woman interrupted her and said "What is wrong with you?" but she didn't respond ... So she began shaking Ashley to the point where she was so scared and wanted to call the ambulance for help. Well, as you can probably guess, Ashley was wrestling with demons and she didn't feel comfortable telling her friend how she felt by her sharing that information. So she finally got up after about 15 mins of wrestling and once Ashley was about to call the police she came back into her senses and she said "let's go". (We have the power to control what we say and do when we let it take advantage of our carnal mind) So they went on, and Ashley's friend kept asking her "what was that" and "what happened to you" but she answered her not a word, and they just started plotting on the next victim. So when they got to a park they saw a woman with her son and started to plot against her to take her son and play with him and then start swinging him around and beating him up to see what the woman would do.

The woman was reading her Bible while her son was playing on the playground equipment so they came over, nearer to him and they felt strange a little bit and started to back up and just as they backed up, Ashley started coughing and coughing uncontrollably; As the woman saw them (with the peak of an eye) and kept reading, she had a feeling that they were about to try and do something. So she kept on reading with her legs crossed, and at this point, she decided not to look up again. The two women were talking, and Ashley was finally able to speak and said a curse word. So her friend asked her "What's up". She said "That kid seems like he had a gleaming light around him or some kind of force where I couldn't even go to play with him "that's crazy" So she insisted, "let me try it again"! A little more eager this time, she went over with a bit more aggression and said "Hey kid, you wanna play?" So as the mother kept her head down, she heard her son say "I wanna play if you wanna play, but then we gotta play my way" And Ashley when she heard it was a little suprised to hear him respond in such confidence like that so she said "Sure.." and she had her fists up to the little boy saying "let's play punching bag" and the boy said "uh-uh, I said we gotta play my way. My way or the highway". Ashley didn't like those words and took it as a threat, and seeing him as a threat and hinderance to their plan, she got kind of scared so she ran over to him as if she were to embrace him on the monkey bars but he flipped up toward heaven and she yelled come here, as she missed him and fell down on her face. She was furious when she got up but said "I know you really wanna play so come down here. Why did you let me fall on my face like that, I was only gonna wrestle with ya". So the little boy stood up on the monkey bars with his fists down to his sides like superman, and he told her "well I don't wanna play like that, let's try something else we both can agree with". So she said "Fine, what do you wanna play then?" The boy's name was Rupert so his mom called him "Rupert, come on it's almost time to go." And he yelled "Mom, please can we stay a little longer?" So she agreed and kept on reading The Word. As he turned back to Ashley, she was already climbing on the monkey bars to meet him up there. So she met him and was considering pushing him off of the high monkey bars but he told her "A little leaven leaveneth the whole lump" and she said "what does that mean?" So he said, "Well, to start off with, when did you first decide to become a bully?"

She laughed at him and said "baby cakes, I ain't no bully I love kids." So he said to her, "Ok, if you "aint no bully" like you say you're not, then why did you plot on pushing me off of the monkey bars when you got up here?" and she responded "well young man I didn't wanna push you off, i just wanted to play," as she then fixed herself in position to push him off while keeping herself up, she leaned foward to push, but there was a crevace that the boy took a hold of to move himself out of her way, so her hand went foward and she fell head first toward the ground again, and this time, it really hurt; Cause that was a long fall. Her friend, standing near the park bathroom was on her cell phone playing candy crush while she was waiting on a que from Ashley. She never got one, but then again, never payed attention to what was going on either. Had her friend known, they would have plotted on another victim a while ago instead of the ones they had. So the boy went on down to check on Ashley as she attempted to get up, trying to decide what to do with him. He said to her "I'm gonna tell you one thing and one thing clear, REPENT".

And though she didn't know exactly the full meaning of the word "Repent" in her spirit she knew exactly what he was saying to her. So Ashley got up and said "I had enough of you for one day". And she walked away. The little boy ran over to his mother once those two women left to tell her all that happened and before he told her she smiled and embraced him saying "Good job baby". So they left. Ashley went on searching for her friend and found her screaming and shouting "High score, woohoo, wassup, wassup,

wassup! (rolling her arms around), and she had so much mulch on herself, dusting herself off onto her friend that her friend looked up at her and asked "What happened to you?" so Ashley replied "Nothing that a good hook up with your ex boyfriend can't fix." So her friend was mad at her after that and said to her "Look, I don't know what happened to you or what your problem is but if I can't entrust you to anything anymore, then what does that make you to me?" and they started arguing back and forth about it until it got dark outside. Ashley was done and still covered in mulch, then they both decided to split ways.

Now, one of the women on her way home decided to take the fast way to her house, in the woods but she didn't want to pass by her ex's way and took the back road once she got to a certain point. Later on that evening she saw on the breaking news channel that a woman in the same part of the woods that she went through, (not too long after she passed there) got raped by a man having on a black leather jacket and timberland boots. So she automatically thought of her friend Ashley, and called her up to apologize and check on her. Meanwhile Ashley was still a little kindled from what just recently happened but answered the phone after a couple of rings. She assured her that she wasn't the rape victim. She told her of how it was the exact same woods at almost the exact time after she passed by when the incident occured. Ashley said "Well why couldn't it have been you then" and her friend just hung up after that.

Ashley's friend later decided after some time since they got off of the phone that they needed some time to be a part for a while and about two days later Ashley calls her friend to ask her if she wants to meet up but she refused. After persistently begging her and asking for forgiveness, the woman eventually gave into the request of her friend to renew there friendship back to the way it was;

so they met up again. Ashley and her friend became close again like they were and they began again to plot and decieve people. It wasn't too long though before they started becoming bored with it and feeling like they wanted more. So they began tricking people out of money and setting themselves up for some grave destruction, It got so bad that they started using witchcraft to get their way, and so they started posing as nuns tricking whoever they could. They told this one guy that if he didn't give his money and car to the "nuns" he would spend the rest of his life in a tomb, then they smeared his face with hot oil telling him lies about the oil being an antidope for the problems that he shared with them. But the young man eventually left the two women in fear and doubt of them then started telling as many people about them as he could. They were getting others to worry in fear (Decieving and being decieved). This lasted for about 2 weeks but it got so bad within that short time that they physically started to change looking as if there physical features were starting to morph. They had been playing around with too much craziness.

Now it was not too long after that when they ran into the young boy again which caused Ashley trouble in the park. This little boy was carrying a small dog with him this time while walking alone near a supermarket. He was in a rural like place of their part of town. Then Ashley said to herself "well he's by himself alone now. I guess he won't be so brave"; but that wasn't the case ... So Ashley quickly met up with him and started mocking and jesting at him to get him upset and to cry. The little boy stood up to her with a smurk and said "You know ... You got a long way to go if you don't turn around now". Ashley knew that he was saying something spiritual to her but she still didn't want to understand. Meanwhile, her friend came up behind the little boy and started shaking him by the shoulders and said "You little fool, you little.. (as she persisted), you don't know anything". So the boy took

Ashley's friend by the hands (as she shook him) and he flipped her over on her back. Ashley then charged straight into him and tried to grab his body to swing him around, but as she dives to embrace his waist, before she could get a good grip of him, he used his two knees to jump up, and kneel her in the face. So she fell on the floor by turning to the side. But she was hurt. Rupert's dog was over nearby a tree with his leash dragging on the ground. He was waiting on Rupert. So Rupert then caught up with his dog and decided to go. "Now one of the women that got hurt yelled out "Aghh aghh you …, ugh … What is with you … "But Rupert and his dog turned away and just sighed. Rebecca cried "Agh Ashley this hurts, I'm so hurt!." Now Rebecca was tall and slim with long dark brown hair, while Ashley was shorter and slender with black hair and bangs. She wore dark lipstick and had a tatoo on her back. Ashley got up then pulled Rebecca up saying "C'mon" we need to go." But Rebecca refused and insisted she was really hurt and wanted to lay there for a few minutes. How did that little boy do that?" "I mean, he's just a kid for crying out loud." Rebecca said to Ashley. And she just stood there shaking her head.

Later after they finally decided to get up and go, they were walking down a dark road in the middle of the street with no cars. It was quiet, and as they started walking, Rebecca started to think things like: Maybe they shouldn't do what they were doing anymore, tricking people. And she started to think; What if it was them that were getting tricked. So she said to Ashley, remember that time the pizza man came to the door and we both saw him and liked him, she said yea … Well I liked him more! Ashley said nu-uh, I liked him more! Then Rebecca said, Ashley what if that same fine pizza man tricked us the way we've been tricking people, how would we feel? She said "Well, never thought of it in that way but that's a good one." "She said also well, you know I have really been thinking about my behaivor lately and how I could change" Rebecca said "Really, how?" So Ashley said "Well for starters, I've been thinking about changing my surroundings and how I could get rid of you." ... & she laughed a little and said "Or getting you a brain" and she laughed some more and then exclaimed to her, "Rebecca, why do you let people move you so easily?, Why are you so fragile and weak?" "What about fun? What about life and living?" "Do you always feel like you wanna give into your inner feelings? Cause if so, then leave me out of it!" And Rebecca cried "Why are you so mean?!" "Do you just think of yourself all the time?" And as they continued walking eventually the both of them just stopped talking and it was so quiet, you could hear the crickets.

Overtime, about a month's space went by and Ashley and Rebecca started to ease off of their usual routine of going out face to face meeting people and just stood home playing games and tricking people on hotline calls. Meanwhile, As each day went by, there wasn't a single day where the woman that Ashley and Rebecca left crying and hurt on the ground that day, didn't pray for them. She started getting even closer to God since that incident and realized some things about herself. And about how it wasn't really her being nice at at all; and that it was really God using her to get His people. That energy that drove her to do those sympathetic things was none other than God Himself, not her! But she wrongingly took credit for the things that God has Blessed her with. Well, she went on her way to get some things from the supermarket oneday, and who did she witness with her 2 eyes? You got it! Rebecca and Ashley. So she immediately went fast out of the car to greet them, and was just so enthused about herself and how much she's changed, and wanted to tell them how since that incident she has been praying for them and that she has changed so much for the better, and when Ashley stopped her in the middle of her speech, She said, "Look woman, if you don't get out of here, we will hurt you Just like we did last time." But the woman kept on trying to convince them until Rebecca said "Wait Ashley, I don't think this is by coincidence that we are meeting her again, and I've been feeling heavy in my Spirit that this stuff weve been doing is not right." So Ashley folded her arms and told the woman that she had until the count of three to leave and she began counting until the woman took off into the supermarket. Rebecca just stood there and then took Ashleys hands down sand to hold them, and said "Look, I know your'e not down for mushy talk; but maybe mushy isn't so bad on you. In fact it spices up your character a little bit more and without it, you just look so dead." Ashley interrupted before she went on and said "Aren't you the one who just did evil with me to all those innocent people?" "And whose shoulder are you gonna run to when you feel bad about those innocent people's heart you just crushed? So you have 2 innocent people you wanna save but yet you've killed all these other peoples, tell me, what difference does that make? That still makes you a cruel heartless woman, and you can't make up for that! So why do you even care about them?!" Rebecca really started to question Ashley and her motives after she said that, and it made Rebecca more keen on getting to know more about all of the things the woman told them.

About 2 years later, the man that delivered the pizza to Ashley's house was now working in his father's owned business called "The Square Garden Inn", which was a huge hotel Corp. that upheld Christian principles, and he was now able to retire from the amount of money they were making. His father upheld these principles by providing his guests with hotel accomodations which influenced scripture and many other things like that which he could think of; and he did very well, but he still wanted to do more and he felt as if there were still some things lacking. Anyway, the pizza man decided to do some online dating to search for a new girlfriend being too shy to talk to women face to face; and he still remembered how those girls made him feel all that while ago when he delivered pizza to him. So he went on for about a few mo.s and he found someone he was interested in called nickname "Misses Cakes", while his online nickname was "Bigshot". So they decided to set a dinner date in one week from that time. He was excited and started working out more and getting close to 175 He thought that he was going to win her heart in no time!

Meanwhile, back at Ashley's house, they were still fooling around when they heard a knock at the door. And who was it? Ashley's mom.. She came in fussing about how they spent all day not cleaning up and messing up the house and how they didn't take out the trash or mow the lawn and she said "What have you 2 grown women been doing all day?" Ashley told her mom "Look, I know things look bad but I just wanna finish up what I'm doing, anyway I know that I'm good enough to get a man and be the boss, … "until her mom interrupted her to say "Be quiet, until you make some sense Ashley!" "You are grown and good enough to get out and make some money. So they both (Ashley and Rebecca,) just left the house before the argument kindled. The pizza man/ or "Bigshot", was still feeling fancy so he decided after working out to go take a peek at his date's inbox to see her messages. *(Now this is not an actual dating site,)* but the dating site is like a game, and on it once you reach a certain amount of trust in your date, you retrieve a key where you can open up there inbox to see there messages. So he read a couple of messages from fans that wrote to his date's inbox. One of the messages said "You are so unique and intriguing, when do I get to know you?" And another one said "GIRL I WANNA BE WITH YOU FOREVER AND A DAY" while another one said "Can I take you out on a date to the movies?" His date hadn't retrieved those messages yet, but he opened them up anyway, so when she saw that they have been read, she was a little dissapointed but she forgave him. She told them that getting to know her isn't easy but that she was very impressed by how he approached her especially considering all of the other approaches that he saw in her inbox and they both laughed about it.

So they spoke from about 12 am till about 5 o clock in the morning; and finally decided to get off of the chat. When they got off he was very pleased, but still wanted to see her because he hadn't seen her yet; (Once they get to a certain level of trust on the site, they can choose to either see thier date on the internet, or take them out to see them in person. So he chose to be patient and wait. He somehow knew it was all worth it. Meanwhile later that day Ashley and Rebecca went to look for other places inside the mall that they could start to play around with people's emotions again instead of on the phone and on the computer. Ashley went on into this clothing store in the mall to try on clothes and she saw this cute red and white dress they had on sale and wanted to try it on, so she did and called in Rebecca saying "Is this cute?" Is this cute enough for my date?" and they laughed and began to make jokes. As they continued, they heard this big huge siren go off from the mall speakers and they told everyone to evacuate the building. So they did, and left the mall shortly after the scene. They later found out it was a bomb threat in the mall and it took them up until about 2 days to make sure that everyone was out and safe; and to make sure that there was no bomb in the mall. But going back, once they (Ashley and Rebecca), left the mall, they decided to go on a long strip near that part of town, that had restaurants, different clubs and bars etc. So Rebecca went in one of the lounges that was there and inside there were different schemes of blue, and blue lights shining from the ceiling, and the decorations were all blue. There were no security guards present or even anyone on the outside to watch. As she was in, she just stood there in awe gazing at the different decorations and saying ooh ahh. Until Ashley came in and grabbed her and said "Will you come on and lets go?" They both went out on their way back home when the security guard shows up saying "wait a minute how old are you 2" Then Ashley, being scared said: "Were old enough to get in for 2 cold drinks on a napkin please" and he just smurked and said "Okay, okay, but no seriously I wanna make it easy for you 2 to get in for free".

So he snatched them up and they went in and ready to go. Meanwhile, "Bigshot" got home from being out that day and realized that his computer wasn't getting any e-mail notifications from his date and it's been quite a while now. He started checking his inbox and checking hers too. She didn't have any new e-mails so he started getting worried thinking "What is she doing" "I wonder if she's chatting with one of the guys I saw in her inbox and he just left it at that till about 2 hours from then, she messages him "Hi are you online?" He didn't answer, but he knew how he was just being stubborn he just felt like he needed something more from her since it's been a while from the last time they chatted but she said no more.

He decided. After 20 mins that he would finally text her back and when he did, she was eager to talk to him and wondered how his day was. She said she wished she could have spoken to him sooner but she got caught up in some work she was doing. He didn't believe her and wanted to know what it was that she was up to (aside from what she told him already). So she gave it a break and told him she was going to talk to him in the morining and that she had a long day. So they both got off and waited until the morning. Well Ashley and Becc had a great time in the club joint and Rebecca has been checking her phone from the time they left out; It wasn't until just then when Ashley asked her who it was that was so important she had to keep checking her phone but

Rebecca said it was her Mom. By the time they left from the place, there were about 5 different guys that wanted to meet Rebecca and take her number but she insisted that she didn't want to be bothered; So Ashley looked at her like she was crazy and instead, she took them all. One of the guys offered to take them home but Rebecca said "No!" Ashley said yes and insisted. Even though it was late, Rebecca was finally regaining sense about herself and told them both that if they wanted to go they could go ahead together, and Ashley remembering the time before when they got into it, decided to walk back home with Rebecca. The guy that offered them a ride home, not too far behind them followed. Ashley dropped Rebecca off this time; (Considering her mom's stance before they left) and then she headed her way. All of a sudden when she gets a little while down the street, she sees these big yellow lights shine on her from the back and the guy stuck his head out of the window screaming "Hey you! remember me?" As he drove closer to her in the middle of the street.

She turned around and said "Go away but he said to her" yea remember yall didn't want that ride, I remember that and he cursed her and yelled "girl!" and he starts riding next to her every footstep, swerving as she's walking. She walks folding her arms with her head down and he starts scooting his car and slamming his brakes in attempt to scare her. He starts teasing her while he's inside the car and threw some old mcdonald's bags at her and she screamed "Go away, leave me alone". But he wouldn't, he just kept on trying to get her to retaliate but she wouldn't, he just kept on trying to get her to retaliate but she wouldn't. She kept ignoring him until she started running. And then he zoomed up beside her again pressing the brakes on his car and pretending like he was going to hit her. So she moved into the grass of someone else's house and walked alongside there and then further up, decided to go into someone's backyard until he left. But he didn't he just pretended he did. He pulled off fast. And somewhere along the road decided to make a u-turn in a place where she couldn't see him. So he parked and got out of the car. He ran behind a few houses then he saw her.

She just kept walking until she got back into the street light again, by this time she was past her house but did not want him to see where she lived so she had already made up in her mind to campout somewhere for a little while. So as the night progressed, Ashley began feeling tired and decided it was time to go inside. Meanwhile, they guy goes back inside the car (Once he found out where she lived) and took off. The next morning "Bigshot" pops up out of his bed and runs to the screen of his computer to check for notifications. And there was his date "Misses Cakes" sending him a "Goodmorning" and "hope you had a good sleep" Text. While he was pondering on what to say to her next, he remembered how the conversation went yesterday and how she said she was busy from earlier in the day so he asked her what it was that she was doing yesterday, He said "If you don't mind me asking, what was it that had you so tied up yesterday?" So she responded "Well, there were a few essays I had to finish up for these short classes that I'm taking. Then, there are a few other things like working out, catching up on bills and etc. that I was taking care of, why?" He said, "Well, I just wanted to know, no biggie." She said "Okay, yea so have you eaten yet?" He replied "My breakfast will be a protien shake and a bannana." "Oh that sounds good" She replied … So they kept on the conversation for about 30 mins this time until they both got started with their day.

Rebecca woke up and started wondering about Ashley and if she made it home okay (seeing as though she didn't reach out to her that night to see if she made it in or not.) Well Ashley decided that she was still uncomfortable going back out the next day for some reason. So she stayed in the house when Rebecca called her at 9 am in the morning, she said "Hey girl whatsup, you make it in okay? And she said "Barely, but If I didn't, it would have been too late … Had I died, how would you have known seeing that you are just now checking up on me?" So they talked for a while and Ashley told her the whole story So Rebecca started wondering how she could've helped and if it were possible, how she could get her to come outside because she missed her and wanted to see her so they could hang out that day. Well, Ashley was adamant about not coming out and Rebecca would have proposed for her to come over but she remembered how Ashley's Mom reacted when she got home and didn't wanna re-kindle the fire. So Rebecca stood home and Ashley stood home. That night, Rebecca had a dream. And in the dream she kept seeing a dark man-like figure circling around her. So she decided to get a drink of water when she woke up. She then went back to sleep and saw it again; it had on all black and was fully clothed in black from head to toe and it's eyes could not be made out. It was circling her and this time, it was hard to circle around her because of this glow that was starting to form around her so the thing had no choice but to back up further and further so the circle got wider and wider as he circled her. And she woke up. By that time it was time for her to get up and go on about her day. So she did, and when she got up, she started to wonder what the dream was about. But she eventually left it alone and hopped on the phone with Ashley again, asking her if she was still determined not to come outside but this time she said no; and that they could hang out once she got out of the shower and did some things. By now "Misses Cakes" Was ready to head on to some other things. She wanted to meet her match and started to get impatient about what it would be like because of what he was saying behind his screen. So she decided to go on ahead and write him that day since the last time they spoke was the previous morning. She asked him how he was doing.

He quickly responded her "I'm doing well, how are you Miss?" and she said "I'm fine thank you" (This time she was on her phone) and she told him that she was waiting on a friend so they could go out and enjoy their day (because the weather was so nice.) He said "Oh really" "And what kind of friend is she?" Misses Cakes told him," Well how do you know that it is a "she"? So he put "Lol :)" and then she waited until he said something else and he just said "It better be". She was touched after that and blushed a little bit. So they began chatting and it was getting closer and closer to the time where they were actually going to go out and meet. As the time passed, "Big shot" just kept getting physically stronger and stronger, He thought it was her that was amping him up so he kept talking to her while he did his workouts. She kept reading her book and texting as she was waiting for her friend; and then her friend came, so she wanted to get off the chat. They would remember this once they decided to get married and have something to laugh about in the end. At least that's what he thought. So Ashley and Rebecca met up and began to do the same things they always do, but this time, they came to a hotel nearby them and went inside.

When they went inside, they decided to start a quarrel with the hotel's front desk clerk, Ashley said to the clerk "We are looking for a room to fit 20 people." So the lady responded "Ma'am is this a party you will be having?" Ashley said "A party? Are we allowed to have parties here?" and the clerk responded "Well, yes we have a ball room, If you would like for me to show you, follow me it is right down this way … "When Ashley interrupted saying "Are you mocking me woman?" and she insisted "No, no no we really have a guest ball room if you would come with me, it is right this way.." And Ashley responded "Get your manager!" "I asked you a simple question you idiot and I expected a simple answer ... I wanted a room, not a ball room!" So the woman was perplexed at Ashley's response and she kept on (While Rebecca was starring at them) "Get your manager NOW!" So the woman said "Sorry ma'am right away." The woman hadn't been working there very long and was around the age of 27 or so. She went to get the manager and before the manager could address the scene, the clerk began to explain in details about the situation so the manager heard the beginning, but then she just shut her up and said "Just show me who she is". (Now the manager was short tempered and self righteous. Her mercy only depended on what she thought was right, she didn't trust God for herself, but was lead by her own opinon and had her own set of morals) They both walked up to Ashley and before they could even get close, Ashley said "Don't test me ... Both of you better keep at least 10 feet away from me." So the manager insisted "Well ma'am, how can you hear us then?" Ashley said "Don't you get smart with me" The manager "What exactly is the problem here Ms.?)

So Ashley told her, "I'm a Mrs. so call me that; and your stupid hotel clerk dared to step to me to ask if I wanted a ball room, After I clearly cried, explaining to her that I needed a room tonight, but she said that no space was available after I told her that I wanted a room for myself and my friend here. I told her that I was short on money and she insisted that we see a ball room that I can't afford so that she could insult me." So Ashley kept on, and insisted that they deserve a free room. Then the manager insisited that they get a free room for 1 night but after that they would have to pay the full price. (They were a customer is always first and right company that stuck to their motto no matter what). So they were thrilled and got their room and started to call people to invite them over. People came and they ordered pizza and chinese food. Then Ashley started with the janitor making demand after demand on the phone with the clerk. She called the janitor every second just to complain about the room because she kept finding "Something" that wasn't right about it. Until finally it was the next day and 12 o clock noon hit. They had partied all that night but everyone was still sleeping at the time. The telephone in the room rang and Ashley was laying right next to it and picked it up "Hello" (With a tired sounding voice)

"Ma'am, It's time for you and your guests to leave the hotel, the checkout time is 12:00." So Ashley slammed down the phone and went back to sleep. There were some people sleeping on the floor and they asked her "Who was that" but she didn't answer so they went back to sleep. After about 20 minutes later they heard a bang at the door. So one of the guests on the floor hopped up and opened it and saw the Manager there with a stern look on her face and she asked for Ashley personally so Ashley got up and said "What? What is it? I'm tired!" and the manager said "What do you mean what is it? "didn't you get my telephone call at 12 o clock Ms?" And Ashley pleaded with her that she was so tired and she didn't want to be bothered so the Manager warned her that if she didn't get her, her guests and her things out of the hotel room by 1 o clock pm then she would call the police. So the woman said "I've been very lenient on you and I've been getting numerous complaints about the party but have spared you and now you are taking too much advantage so I'm going to have to call the police if you and your guests are not out by that time" She said "Okay, okay okay I got it just please let me sleep." And the manager said "I have warned you" and she left.

So Ashley went back to sleep while her guests decided that after that, it was time to leave. When she woke back up it was 12:59 and it was only her and Rebecca when they heard a knock at the door. Ashley got mad then and said "What?! Is it?!" and the manager just came on in this time with her access key and she was with the police, she said "I've told you, I was merciful to you and I even gave you a complimentary night because of your complaint that made no since" "So now I'm leaving it up to the officials to let them be your judge". So Ashley woke up and said "Alright well get out, well leave it's fine well leave. Since you want it that way" And they gathered their things and left". The police pulled Ashley aside and spoke to her saying "You know I have every right to place you in cuffs and put you away for your inconsiderate disturbances" She said" Well, whatever it is sir, I'm sorry" "I don't know what she told you, but it's not true, you see, I had a long day the previous day and I asked the woman very nicely if we could stay there, and I cried and fought hard and tried to stay there for that night so we could have the party but she told me that I was a loser and a scumbag that's why I needed to go and find a different hotel."

"Sir she was very mean even though she's pretending to be nice now, and that is why after my complaining she decided to give us a room" "So he said to her "Oh I didn't know that was what it was, I'm sorry ma'am, you shouldn't have gotten treated this way if that was the case. Are you sure that's what happened?" She insisted and said "You see officer, everything that glitters aint gold, have you heard of that before?" He said "Well, yes I have ma'am, but anyway I want to make sure that you get everything you need so incase you have any other problems, here's my card" She said "Thank you sir" and she winked at him. So they left the hotel and the manager there decided that she wouldn't show mercy anymore to people and she started to change as a person, (but her character was becoming created and manipulated because of what she experienced rather than pruned and sharpened and turned to God), After she found out what Ashley said to the police she tried to get pictures of them on camera when they were standing at the front desk to ban them from coming back, And the company then changed their mottos.

As time and time went on Ashley kept seeing Rebecca on her phone and she wondered why she was spending so much time on it at the hotel so she asked her. And Rebecca replied to her "If you only knew what I was doing, you would be so upset" "So she said No, what? tell me!" She was starting to adapt Ashley's ways but she knew how to control it and when to stop so that was acceptable to her. The problem was since her ways imposed so much on Rebecca's character, and being that they were so close, she wanted to, and thought she could control it whenever she wanted, but she really actually couldn't. That was the deep rooted deciet Rebecca was entraped in. So Ashley asked her again "What is it, what is it?!" But Rebecca wouldn't tell her who it was she was spending all her time with on that phone. So she eventually let it go as they went on. They started scamming old men out of their wealth and practicing sorcery and tricks on their old women. "Ashley do you feel bad about what happened back at the hotel at all?" "NO" Ashley said.

Well what about the guy who followed you home, what if he did something to you? "So ... " She said. Well.. "Rebecca be quiet! Why do you always have to fight me?" Everything was starting to happen for Rebecca's benefit due to Ashley's arrogance and pushing her way through life by herself. So Ashley began to tell Rebecca about herself some more so the issue wouldn't arise again.. she said "The only reason you get all of these great benefits and all the laughs throughout the day are because of me and what I do for you. I don't see you talk to anyone or approach anyone when we go out or meddle, no, all you do is get the laughs and enjoyment, you don't break a sweat my dear!" And here you are sitting looking all pretty twirling your hair and biting your fingernails while I do all the work and meet all of the people. You are just as bad as a stuffed animal that has no life in it!" So Rebecca just sat there and listened until she was done. Then she said "Ashley, you know what?" I'm getting tired of you surrounding me with lies and coming up with all of these accusations against me and against other people." "Well, my friend, what are you gonna do about it?" So Rebecca left to her house.

Immediately when Rebecca got home she got on her phone and started chatting, but this time she was grieved. Something moved her to cry as she was chatting with the mysterious person. She was crying crying and couldn't stop crying until the person on the phone said "What's wrong? You seem a little different tonight" and Rebecca said "I had a dream. In my dream there was this big black thing with no eyes that kept circling me round and around so I woke up and didn't know what it was. When I went back to sleep, That same black thing came and it was like I felt a big bubble around me and that thing had to back up but it was still circling around and around me, it just had a limit as far as how close it could be around me. I don't know what that dream means. So the mysterious person said "Whoa, maybe you should call a doctor" but Rebecca knew that a doctor couldn't do much about her dream and she just kept crying and didn't bother texting anymore.

As she cried, she ended up going to sleep and missing out on all the texts she was getting but she didn't care. So as she slept, she had the same dream over again and this time the black figure was crying while flying and circling around her. When she woke up, she remembered what she said to Ashley. She told Ashley that she was tired of her surrounding her with lies, so she began to get worried and wondering what was actually happening and if the dreams were significant to what was actually happening in real life. So Rebecca started to cry again and panic and she went into this deep silence and avoided Ashley for about 4 weeks (which was very uncommon for her being as though they spent time together almost everyday) Until the point when Ashley was willing to do anything to get her normal friendship back. She kept telling her sorry and sending things by her mother to give to her but Rebecca would not budge. During that time period, Ashley had shaved off her hair, got rid of her make-up and tatoo and made a tatoo of Rebecca's name. While Rebecca, well she actually started to want to get close to God. She began thinking about what that woman told them. The one that saw them at the super market, Rebecca wanted to know what she was all about. She said, "God, are you here? If so, please help me understand all these things that are going on." The very next day, God did help her understand much. So much that she permanently seperated ways from her friend Ashley.

God began to show Rebecca her purpose from the beginning of her life until now and why she was so easily persuaded by Ashley and why she didn't care about life. He started to show her about Ashley and how she was resistant to change for the better. She even saw that the dream she had was about Ashley. It was figurative for what was happening in her life. The dark figure that circled around Rebecca was a spiritual figure that represented Ashley's dark soul. The reason why it kept going at a further distance from Rebecca is because Rebecca was about to soon break free from that manipulative bondage of influence that Ashley held over her life. That spirit Ashley was following would soon to be unable to manipulate and control Rebecca, being as though she would now find Christ! There were so many things that were shown to Rebecca that day and throught the night, that Rebecca ended up changing her number, giving up a lot of things she used to do, and she completely turned around and gave her life to Christ. She went through withdrawl from not seeing her friend Ashley, but in the end it was all worth it. She started to have other dreams of that same dark figure and it was pertaining to the things that would soon happen to Ashley had she not changed. But, she also had numerous dreams and visions pertaining to things that would actually happen in life reguarding the future of the World. She didn't know how to handle all of the dreams she was having but she kept relying on God and gradually, He showed her what to do at His time. Meanwhile, back at "Mr. Bigshot's" crib, he was tired and relaxed but had stopped talking to "Miss Cakes" for a while now because he was a little nervous considering that he would be meeting her in 2 days. He tried to put on his best front to make it seem like he was cool about meeting up with her. She couldn't keep her cool so she ended up calling him and he answered and she said "You know were meeting up in 2 days right?" So he said, "Yea" "And it's a lovely thing to finally hear your voice" (He was shocked that she was brave enough to call him being as though they hadn't talked on the phone yet.) So she said "Are you suprised to hear me, to hear my voice?" He said "Yea you sound so beautiful and full of life, just like I imagined". So she smiled behind the phone and said "Well I can't wait for these 2 days to hurry up and pass because I can just imagine the stature behind a voice so strong and unique." They both began to be a little bit on edge at that point in seeing eachother and wanted the time to hurry up and pass. They wanted to pick out some nice outfits to meet up.

"Misses Cakes" decided to shop around and see what outifits they would have at the mall while "Bigshot" wanted to see what he could get online in a business day. So as they both shopped and shopped around for what things they could wear, 1 day went past and they were able to finally find an outfit that each of them liked. Miss Cakes was ready to tell him some things that happened to her in her past that he didn't know about during the time period of them talking. While "Big shot" Was ready to talk about marriage. He knew what he wanted and didn't have to search around. He didn't have to see her, he knew she was his. His father's owned business made him very well rounded about life because he got a chance to travel and meet people and learn alot of different things. she had a few well rounded experiences too, considering that she was in control of her own ministries all around the world. Now another day went by and during this time, Ashley was really starting to worry about Rebecca. She hadn't seen her in so long and wondered what had happened to her, and why she wasn't answering her calls. She went by on several occasions but Rebecca would not even come out of her room when Ashley was at the door. So Ashley finally gave up and decided she didn't know what was wrong with Rebecca and she was gonna go and find someone else to cause trouble with. One day, Ashley went into a supermarket that was on a strip near were there were several different restaurants, so before she went in, she passed this one restaurant in particular named "The wind"

So she decided to take a peek inside there because it smelled really good and on the outside it looked beautiful. So Ashley said "Ooooh it smells goooood." As she walked past everything until the front desk Usher said "Can I help you ma'am" She said, "No" I just wanted to see what it looked like in here. (She wasn't dressed for the occassion.) So he said, "Well Ms, unless you have another pair of shoes and a different wardrobe, you are not permitted in this place, boots are not allowed in here." So she got sassy with the clerk and told him to back off and that anything she wore was permitted in there. So they began to go back and forth for a little while until She spots "The pizza man" or Mr. "Big shots" on his way in and she immediately recognized him and said "Well hello, you look nice" I remember you from a long time ago wow!" So he says, "Hi how are you, I'm not sure I remember your face but anyway it was nice to meet you" as he continues to walk inside. He was so anxious about meeting his date that he didn't recognize her or even take the time to talk to her. So Ashley then decided to get a table after begging the same man that she got smart with, to get one. Insisting that she would walk in there barefoot if she had to. So he agreed to it but told her that she would have to pay "an additional 15 dollars" for "improper attire". So she agreed and went inside. She asked the waitress for a table next to the pizza man but the only one that they could find was a seat spotted next to the window about 5 tables away from him.

So she ordered her drink and kept glancing over at him and wanted to see what his date looked like. As soon as his date arrived, the waitress walked back up in front of Ashley and said "Hello how are you doing ma'am are you ready to order" and Ashley said to her, "Excuse me, but you're blocking my view." So the date came and sat with her back facing Ashley and all she was able to see was the back of her hair. So Ashley ordered anyway, she ordered from the kids menu and to her suprise they had pizza and fries. So she ordered the pizza and fries and the waiter left the table. Ashley kept trying to look over to see the girl when suddenly, a man walks over to introduce himself. He starts talking to her and telling her how she was beautiful and how he loved her attire. So Ashley let him sit (because she figured out a plan to involve him) and when he sat, she just kept looking over his shoulder as he was speaking because he was blocking her view; So she didnt even get his name at the time. He just kept right along talking and she didn't hear a word he said.

So eventually she started to pay attention and talk back to him, after he said to her "Do you know that you can have everything you want for free, if you just pay attention?" at this point she started again to pay attention back over at the pizza man's table and was a little annoyed at the gentleman sitting there with her; but didn't tell him to leave, she just kept trying to see the guy and his date. He went on … "People miss the point of who they are just by going after the things that seem to make them temporarily happy" … & He went on to say "They even go as far as to use mind games to trick people due to their own insecurities and things they think they can't attain. Spiritual things don't make sense to them." And at that point she was a little confused and looked back at him and said "What do you mean they don't make sense to you?" Are you saying Spiritual things don't make sense to you?" He said "Ashley, you are playing with fire, and have been for a long time now. Don't you know that since you came in, your whole focus has been on things of the flesh all the while?" "What you see, what your hands can hold and eyes can grasp?" "The blind have more access to the things of the Spirit than those that can see" The man said. She said "Really?" "Well what I see, I want and what I want, I get." And he said it again "Ashley, you are playing with fire" So Ashley refused to pay any more attention to him at that point because she knew she wouldn't "Win" the conversation. Anything that she couldn't win or have her way in, she didn't like. She took the man as a threat and tried to go around everything he was saying because she didn't want to accept the truth. So eventually the man got up and left and Ashley decided to forget the scheme she would play with the man seeing that she thought he was annoying.

So she eventually got up and decided to walk past them to go to the bathroom. That way on her way back, she would see the woman's face. But as she was on her way back, the woman had gotten up to go to the front desk and Ashley didn't see her or where she had went. So she sat back down. And the woman came not long after Ashley sat down and sat back down too. Ashley was frustrated at this point. So the two talked and were so intrigued with one another that he said to her "Where have you been all this time?" "I've been looking for you!" and she was so fascinated by him that she just laughed. They shared stories about their lives to one another and he ended up telling her the story of when he was a pizza man and 2 girls harrassed him (not knowing Ashley was there). And once she heard the story, she said "Oh, interesting! She was kind of embarrassed not knowing what he would say next and she hopped up out of the chair and said "Excuse me a moment" and ran to the bathroom. Not too long after that, Ashley recieved a phone call from Rebecca. So she left the table, didn't pay for her food or even eat it and ran out of the restaurant. Ashley picked up the phone without even allowing Rebecca to speak, she said "Rebecca, Rebecca, guess what!?

Guess who I just saw! Do you remember the pizza man that came that was so fine a few years back and we spoke to him? well I just saw him on a date, with a girl but I couldn't see the woman I just saw her long black hair like you." Rebecca said "I was just calling to tell you that I've changed, I've changed alot and there are some different things going on with me at the moment" "I've found The Lord Ashley" ... And Rebecca interrupted her and said "Rebecca, I know, I know, just come meet me at this restaurant about a 7 minute drive from your house called "The wind". "Your mom can bring you, it's important" So Rebecca said, don't you think what I'm telling you is important" And Ashley said "Well, no, not right now" So Rebecca hung up the phone; While Ashley persistently tried to call her back, she wouldn't answer. Meanwhile, the date (Miss Cakes) came back to the table and sat down, and Ashley flew back inside. (Again, she saw the date with her back facing Ashley and so she couldn't see her), then the 2 started talking about how Miss Cakes found The Lord and so many other things that have happened to her in her life.

"Big shot" Was so in love with her at this point (At least he thought) and he just kept listening as she spoke and told him things like she didn't want to be alone but not willing to risk her relationship with a man for her relationship with The Lord and he agreed that, that was a good thing. So he told her how his grandmother was in a church that he used to go to but didn't attend often, and she told him. "That is a great thing, but you know something I learned is that it really isn't all about church, I went to churches before and couldn't seem to find one that was just right for me but then at one point I just stopped" "Me too" He said ... and she continued, "Yea, it just felt uncomfortable for me and I didn't go anymore but something happened to me recently where God completely changed my life and not to say He hasn't before, but he just brought me to a truly deeper understanding of who He is and why we are here." I could go on for hours" and he said "I'm listening." "Well, so many people want to go around God to create their own experience of things and to make their own ideas come to life not fully realizing where those ideas come from." "Interesting" He said.. "Yea, these ideas are not uncommon to what God has already planned out for us, it's just up to us to look to Him." He said "Wow, I never thought of it like that" and he went on to tell her about his business and how his dad didn't really know The Lord but wanted to get them into a Christian founded company that stood on Christian principles. So she said "Ooooh is that so?" He said "Yes" and in fact, we are thinking about starting the process now. So she agreed that it was a good idea and let him in on a few tips that would help him excel in him and his dad's business. The date didn't end until the restaurant closed at 3 am and Ashley had left before that time and persistently tried calling Rebecca back to come to that restaurant with her; and even did so much as to walk to her house. But she went home after no one answered Rebecca's door. "Big shot" and

"Miss Cakes" wanted to go on and on talking but it was getting really late or (early) at that time. He was so appreciative with her sharing that information because it would save him and his dad a whole lot of time getting started with the process of change and make them truly excell in the business that business.

So eventually when Ashley figured out that she wouldn't get Rebecca in that way, She decided another method to use. She caught her mom coming outside getting into her van so she stopped her and told her how it really hurt her that Rebecca wouldn't talk to her anymore, and she told her how she has changed and she even went as far as to say that she found God and that she is a new person and how there were some different things going on with her that she wanted to share with Rebecca. So she asked her mom "Why won't Rebecca speak to me?" And Rebecca's mom then replied to her "Ashley, out of all the time I have known you, I've always wanted for Rebecca to have better friends. You have influenced her so much in a negative way and I've always wanted more for her. But she chose to stay around you and she always told me how there was something different about you, and how you were bold and unafraid. Rebecca didn't have that boldness in her and she wanted to share in that with you.

She also told me about how heavily influenced she was to do things that she didn't necc. wanna do but being around you just made her wanna do things and influence just took her over so that she began to like being around you too much and she didn't care … "Her mother goes on to say "She started back-talking me and talking to that boyfriend of hers that I really couldn't stand" "And I'm not saying it was because of you, but I just know how you have held too much influence on her and her life, and it has weighed me down, so when she told me that she has changed and found The Lord in her life, I was so grateful that I didn't know what to do. I just cried. She told me that she also would have to stop hanging around you and she let me in on alot of secrets between you and her of the wicked things you all have done." "So Ashley, it is a great thing if you have found The Lord and I encourage you to continue on your journey and to continue seeking Him, but as of now, please leave me and my daughter alone." "I don't think that she wants to be bothered and I want her to get all of the time she needs to spend getting a relationship with God." and she ended it there.

So Ashley walked away sad and hurt without knowing what to do. Thinking how she would never be able to speak to Rebecca again. Now Rebecca's mom wasn't merciless, so as Ashley continued to walk, she pulled up beside her and said "You know, you are a great girl, fun to be around and full of new ideas … I'm sure oneday whenever God sees fit, you two will be at it again but right now you are going through a stage of pruning and getting to know The Lord, so just wait." Get closer to him during this time.. and she had an extra Bible in her van so she gave it to Ashley and told her "look, read some verses in Matthew, Mark, Luke and John.. And read Romans too. Those verses have been helping Rebecca out alot on her walk, and before you do, Pray." Rebecca's mom knew that she wasn't really trying to get close to The Lord but she thought that it would be of some encouragement to her. So she left her at that point and Ashley respected her mom enough to keep the Bible with her and she walked home. Later on that night Rebecca got into one of her fits and started tossing and turning in her bed. She was having a nightmare and she woke up mad (instead of scared) and she just felt like she wanted to hit somebody.

So she punched the wall near her headboard of her bed and started screaming as if she was going crazy. She couldn't control herself and she started ripping up some of her and Rebecca's pictures they had together and clothes she borrowed from her (This was at 12 o clock in the morning) and books and she was about to throw the Bible but then her mom came in and said "What is going on with you?!" And Ashley started cursing at her mom and saying the first things she could think of when her mom stopped her and said "You know what, if you say another word against me, me and you will have to leave" So Ashley just kept screaming and telling her mom that she didn't understand so her mom said, "I understand very well, you are well over 18 years old and very capable of controlling your temper." I don't know what's happened with you or gotten into you but you really need to get yourself together and do it fast. Then she left and slammed the door.

A few days later, "Big shot" and "Miss Cakes" started talking on the phone and "Big shot" didn't want to waste any more time on getting married to "Miss Cakes" So he decided to purchase a ring for her. He tried to remember what size her hand was, but all he could remember was that it was small, so he asked the cashier for the smallest ring he could find in hopes that it would fit her. So the man gave him a size 6. It was one of the most expensive and beautiful rings he saw there and He said, "This is the one". So the cashier asked him "I bet this is for someone special?" and he answered "You bet it is, I'm going to get married to her and I know she's the one!" He asked "Have you ever thought of the best places to propose, whether somewhere public, or if it would be better somewhere private?" and "Big shot" answered "You know that is a good question, I didn't think of that. My idea was to just do it right on the spot and whatever comes to mind is what needed to be said at the time." So the cashier said to him "Good answer". and they both smiled as Big shot went away and said "Thank you so much sir". Mr. Big shot was at the corner of Misses Cakes' street one evening and he saw her pull in to her home. He ran up to her door and said "Hey, how ya doing Miss?" and she was shocked to see him there because they had just recently got off the phone and she said "What are you doing here?" and he said, "Do you mind if I take you out for a ride?" (Because he saw that she wasn't comfortable with him suprising her there and he got nervous and didn't feel like it was perfect). She said, "Okay just let me bring my bags in the house and I'll be out". She had no idea of what he was going to do considering they hadn't been talking long, she wouldn't expect him to propose to her so soon. But he knew what he wanted. So she went inside and he helped bring her bags inside, then they both left.

Ashley was still trying to reach Rebecca at this time and she kept having nightmares every night, but couldn't find it in herself to submit herself to do what was right. So she decided that she was going to take it a step further and spy on Rebecca to see if she could catch her out oneday and perhaps, talk to her then. But then she remembered how Rebecca wasn't even coming out of her house most of the time. So she decided to try and plan a way to snatch her up take her hostage. She thought to herself "Well she just has to come out oneday." and she began to come up with a plan. She was gonna catch her and drug her up, tie her hands and take her to the cemetery to try and "teach her a lesson." She had so many crazy ideas in her head of what to do and she just started to put them all together. Once she caught Rebecca, she would finally show how she "needed Ashley" and that way Ashley wouldn't be alone. Now the "couple" ended up driving to this beach that was about 3 hours away from Misses Cakes home. And when they got there, it was evening and dark; but the boardwalk of the beach was lit and there were not very many people. So they decided to take a walk on the boardwalk and conversate.

It was a little chilly so Bigshot put his jacket around Misses Cakes and they were walking and talking while all of the shops were closed. She insisted how she wanted to go home after they had left there and he said "Sure! Absolutely I will be taking you home once we leave here." So they found a well lit spot on the beach and they just sat down, talked and laughed and watched the water. They spoke about how The Lord made the sea and how the water stopped right where He made it stop. How the fishes and all of the sea creatures were swimming to and fro trying to get to their destination just like we do in life. They wondered if they had traffic and crossing guards underneath the sea and they thought it was funny. They were talking about the Marines and the Navy and how they get to explore the ocean; and how someday he wanted to as well. He thought about proposing there, but then he saw her face with his jacket wrapped around her, and remembered she was cold. So he said that might not be a good idea.

He then walked her back to his car and they sat there for a while and he turned on the heat. He suggested to her that maybe they should go to a restaurant (seeing that he was getting a little nervous because it was getting late, it was around 11:00.) She said "Okay, well I'm not hungry but we can go that's no problem." So he changed his mind and decided to go to the movies. Once they got there, he changed his mind again, thinking it wasn't a good idea with so many people and the theater being loud etc. So he said, well on second thought, lets just stay in my car and talk. So she insisted to know what was going on with him that he wanted to keep going from one place to another in such a short period of time. She told him "Time isn't going anywhere with us, we plan on seeing eachother more often right?" … "Yes" He said. He said "I just want you to be comfortable." So she assured him "I am comfortable around you wherever we are."

He insisted that they go and head back on their side of town. So they did and close to the time they got back, it was morning. He was driving and watching the sunrise while she was asleep. He was driving over a bridge and about halfway on the bridge he stopped to take a picture with his phone. He took a picture of the sunrise and he also took a picture of her sleeping (not being sure if she would like that or not.) So she woke up realizing they had stopped and she said, "What's going on?" He said "It's warm outside, you wanna come out and see this with me" She said "sure". So she got out and watched the sunset over the bridge and the water. "This is nice" She said.. So he was comfortable and on the bridge he decided that it was time so he got on one knee and reached in his pocket and he proposed to her. Being completely shocked and stunned, She said yes! "So this is why you have been walking around taking me everywhere?" She said.. "Wow you are a charm, I'm going to marry a charmer" She said. After they each went home to freshen up, they spent the rest of that day together.

So later on … Rebecca was going out to the store to get a couple of things that her mom told her to buy from the market. As she got there, she noticed that she forgot her things from the van that she needed to get the things. So she walked back up to the van and saw that one of the tires were flat in the back and said, "hmmm, I didn't notice this before let me call my mom." So she looked for her phone and couldn't find it. So she thought she might have left it at home and said to herself "Well, I guess I'll tell my mom about it when I get back." So she got her card, and the money from out of the van and started walking back into the store. Not realizing that Ashley was in a car (that she had stolen), close by the van. She was sitting there, watching her every move waiting for a perfect chance to get her in the car. So Rebecca did her shopping and came out once she was done only to find out that all of her mom's belongings inside the car were on the ground and every tire was then flat on the van. And she was thinking "What in the world is going on?" So she was afraid to get in the van seeing that the side doors were left open. So she stood there with the groceries in her hand trying to decide what to do.

So Ashley came up behind her with a mask on and a gun directing her to the car and put her inside the car. She was so close upon her that it was hard for anybody to tell that she had a gun against her back. And she told her to walk inside the car and get in. But she felt the cold gun press upon her skin, and she shoved it against her back as she pushed her in the front seat of the car. So Rebecca got sat down and was upset wondering what was going on. Ashley made sure she was secure and couldn't get out and that all the doors were locked. Once Ashely got in, she took off the black mask and said "Hey girl aren't you excited to see me?" Rebecca was shocked and said "NO!" and dropped her groceries as Ashley took off Rebecca was screaming "let me out, let me out!" And Ashley went speeding around the parking lot to get to her destination. She decided to take her to an open space place near a railroad track. So when she got there she told her to "Get out! Since you wanna go" and Rebecca couldn't open the door so Ashley went to the other side of it and opened it up and said "Come on Rebecca, I'm not gonna hurt you "while she had the gun swinging with her hand." So Rebecca got out with her hands up and said, "look Ashley, I don't know what your up to but whatever I did, I am sorry. Look, I've confessed my sins to my Maker and He is the one who will justify me!" So Ashley said ...

"Really ...? Will He justify you when you did evil on all those innocent people and hurt them just like I'm hurting you now?" Rebecca said, "Well Ashley He can save you too ... " but before she could finish Ashley cut her off and told her not to speak anymore. I don't wanna hear it Rebecca, right now I just wanna play." So Ashley put Rebecca on her knees facing the train track and the train was coming so she said "You see that, do you wanna go there?" And Rebecca said, "yea I see it." So Ashley told her to get up and walked her close to the tracks until they got up there and she said "Get back on your knees" So she did and just watched the train pass. meanwhile, the phone was on the ground underneath the van back at the supermarket when Rebecca's mom repeatedly call her to check on her and make sure she was alright. Her mom felt something in her Spirit that wasn't right and called to check on Rebecca. So the phone was left under the van to keep ringing. Back at the scene of Ashley she put a blindfold around her and told her to do many weird things with her strange things she started coming up with, until suddenly She heard footsteps and laughing so she took Rebecca back to the car until she could see who it was, but she didn't see anyone.

And after she thought they had passed and didn't hear anyone anymore, she hopped back out of the car with Rebecca and brought her back to the railroad tracks with her hands tied and a bandana blindfold on her eyes telling her to look and see what the train would do to her so Rebecca replied "I can't see anything, and Ashley came up close to her while she was down on her knees and started touching and rubbing her hair and said "I said look!" Then she smacked her across her face until Rebecca started to cry. And she didn't respond after that but just cried. There were some trees nearby the scene and those voices of laughter were behind them, watching what was going on from the time they had gotten out of the car. So Ashley took Rebecca by the hair and and snatched it and started trying to pull her by the hair against the train track but she was too heavy; So she took her by the arm and told her to get up while she had the gun pointed at her. She then took the blindfolds off of Rebecca and said to her "Do you wanna be my friend?" And Rebecca replied "NO!" (At this time Rebecca was on the train tracks) So she asked her again. "Are you sure you don't wanna be my friend Rebecca?" So Rebecca replied boldly at this point and said "Had you considered turning to God and changing your ways, not showing yourself to be a maniac, I would have considered being your friend again, but at this point Ashley, NO!, and at this point, I don't care anymore!" So one person came from behind the tree with a gun pointed to Ashley telling her to remove Rebecca from off of the train tracks carefully. So Ashley said "Wow, look Rebecca! and took the blindfolds off of her and said "It's the pizza man!" So she snatched her off of the train tracks and did what he said; and as he walked closer to Ashley with the gun still remained at her head, he said "Don't I know you?" And she said to him "Yes, (with a huge smile on her face) and said I know you too and she reminded him of the time he was a pizza man and came to her door" So he thought about it after she reminded him.

Still with the gun pointed at her head, he said "Yea I do remember you both" I remember how I felt so uncomfortable that day; And even though I felt good afterward, I didn't like the way I was seduced by you 2, it kept me blinded for too long to what women should be like. Because of women like you, I never trusted women or took the time to get to understand them, thanks alot! ... But I see your friend changed ... I overheard her talk about The Lord and tell you that you need to change. But you, you are still the same, and now since she's in a good state of mind, you're trying to hold her back aren't you? "So Ashley said "NO!, I was just trying to ... " He smacked her in the face and said "Save it!" Then after seeing that he hit her in the face, his date "Misses Cakes" Rushes over to where they were from behind the tree and said, "What did you do that for, what happened?" And Ashley saw her and said "Hey I remember you!" Miss Cakes said "I remember you too and turned to Bigshot and told him "These are the two girls

I was telling you about that that I recently saw at the market and told them about how God could save them from what they did to me, and from their sins but they wouldn't listen. The same ones that previously set tacs on the ground and beat me up out in the open then I had to go home without going to the store ... but.. This is not a coincidence."

She went on directing her tone towards Ashley saying "And what is the matter that you have your friend here tied up like that?" ... But Ashley didn't respond and they were all shocked at this point. Him with the gun still pointed at Ashley, he thought that she might try something slick because she still had the gun in her hand held down; he told her to "DROP THE GUN." And she dropped it and said, "It was all her fault, she didn't wanna submit to do the right thing so I tried to teach her a lesson" Seeing that she couldn't lie at this point, she made an attempt to escape so she ran fast, in thinking that he wouldn't shoot her, he aimed at a tree and missed her on purpose as she tried to run. She became scared and just stood there. He told her to come back slowly. So she backed up all the way back to the place they were at and he grabbed her by the neck of her shirt and demanded that she come with them and get in the car. At this point, Rebecca was still tied up without the blindfolds but she could walk and Misses cakes said "Come with us, to see the end of this." And so she did. She came with them and they tied Ashley's hands behind her back and sat her in the front of the car with "Bigshot", and Rebecca sat in the back with Miss Cakes.

So he asked Ashley "Where did you get the car from? is it yours?" So Ashley was irritated at that point and said "That's none of your business" and he said to her "Consider yourself Blessed that I'm in my right mind, because if I wasn't right now I would give you a taste of your own medicine, you!" And he cursed her ... So Miss

Cakes called him "Honey". Ashley said "Oh so I see you guys are "Honey's now, you could've been my honey, me and Rebecca would have served you up." So Miss Cakes answered politely, "Well If God saw it fit, I think Rebecca would have been the one to have first dibbs seeing that she's the sensible one." Ashley said.. "What's the problem woman it's not like you 2 are married! You're telling me about God but your probably commiting adultery around with eachother in your mom's basement, what does that make you? So don't come to me and tell me about God." The woman said to her "For someone so beautiful and petite of stature, you sure have a boldness of Spirit in you, but it is the wrong one. We are getting married tomorrow to answer your question.." "It wasn't a question!" Ashley interrupted her. She repeated "Were actually getting married tomorrow and we didn't wanna waste time, but to answer your question, God didn't see it fit that we should be together before marriage, so we accepted the call placed on our life.

Also, things happened so perfect that we didn't waste time to get married and we both knew what we wanted. The same thing could happen for you if you would give God a chance. "You see, things happen for a reason and sometimes we don't know what that reason is until after we make the leap of faith. Everything is ordered and structured by God who makes the steps for us to be successful in all we do if we follow Him. Now, this meeting up happened for a reason too, and only God knows the cause. While we try to figure it out, it will be revealed in due time." But until then, it would be good if you keep your mouth remained closed while were on this trip to jail, seeing you will have alot of time to think and consider doing right and turning your life around to Christ. Getting to know Him." She ended it there and Rebecca came in and said, "Ashley, do you remember when I was on the phone all those times, while we were at the house, in the hotel

and everything?" Ashley said "Yea, so what?" She told her ...
"Well I was talking on the phone to my ex-boyfriend, you know
the one." Ashley screamed "What!?" but she continued.." Well
yea, he raped that woman that you we saw on the news that day
right after we both made it in the house safe, it was him." Ashley
said "So wait, you were still talking to him after that?" She said
"Yea, I was ... " She continued "I was guiding him, he needed a
lot of consolation to get to his right mind after what he did and
he didn't think he would get caught but once he saw his face on
the t.v screen as a criminal, it did something to totally change his
mind about everything he just did, and he started looking for a
way out. So I told him about Jesus!" Ashley didn't say anymore
after that and just remained quiet for the rest of the ride.

Miss cakes and Rebecca began to talk about life and The Lord
and how Rebecca saw how she had been forgiven and Miss cakes
hugged Rebecca as she apologized to her in deep sorrow and asked
her for forgiveness for what her and Ashley had done to her. She
just consoled Rebecca and ensured her that she was on the right
track and to keep going. But Ashley said not a word for the rest
of the ride. On the ride, more and more secrets got revealed. And
they kept conversing, Miss cakes told Rebecca how she used to be
religous and think that she was righteous, even when she cursed
at them, she was religous in her own mind. Though, that was
during the time when she was trying to get to know The Lord
and directed back to Ashley telling her how she should really pay
more attention to how she affects people because it only gets worse
and worse if she keeps going down that road. She spoke about
how The Lord delievered and healed her from that self-righteous
mentality. And Rebecca told her how The Lord showed her it is
effortless. It is an effortless work to be saved because we aren't
worthy and if we are in a position of pruning, it is because of our
stretch of faith. And Miss Cakes was very excited to hear Rebecca

say that, it brought her comfort and confirmation to Rebecca's witness of getting to know The Lord. And she invited her to the wedding. She told her how that in a matter of a day, they were able to find the people who were suitable for the wedding (seeing how "Bigshot" already had some people prepared before he purchased the ring) all she had to do was call and tell people on her side and it worked out perfectly because the people that she invited were free to attend. Rebecca then smiled at her and said "Yes that is perfect"

They finally arrived at the station and "Big shot" told Ashley to "Get out".. So they all got out and walked inside the station to explain the matter. After the 3 left the station without Ashley, they drove back to Rebecca's house and once they got there, Miss Cakes handed her the invitation of where to be tommorow, so they said goodbye to eachother and took off. Now Rebecca walked in the house to her mom saying "Where were you?" and she was worried about her long trip to the store. She wondered what had happened to her and why she wasn't answering her phone and that's when Rebecca remembered and said "My phone!." (But she didn't want to explain the issue of her meeting up with Miss Cakes and told them to go without coming in to meet her mother. Even though she had revealed many things to her mom during her walk with The Lord, she didn't want her new friends getting in the mix, (at least not yet, and she just felt uncomfortable.) So she told her mom that she would tell her everything that happened but she needed to run back to the store to get her phone. So this time she caught a cab back to the market, hoping that everything was still in it's place and that the wind didn't blow everything away during the time that she was gone. And when she got there, she saw everything as a beautiful mess, lying on the ground, untouched like it was before she left. So she searched for the phone inside of the van but then it started ringing. She heard it and realized that it was underneath the van, so she crawled underneath to get it and after she did that, put all of her belongings back inside of the van. Then she said a prayer and took off back to the house. Misses Cakes and Bigshot's number was on the back of the invitation. As soon as she pulled up home, she called them to thank them once again for saving what could have been her life.

On the phone, "Miss Cakes" or Natalie, told her how God showed her personally that right and wrong morals don't depend on what we go through because God doesn't change His standards according to our situations here on earth, He grants us mercy according to His standards. She continues ... "He shows us through Jesus' Holy Spirit, how to handle our personal situations. "Right and wrong is only a matter of knowing God and what He says is right or wrong, she said. I was enslaved to my own mentality that I've built by my own standards. Spending so much time thinking that I was justified by my own right doing and what I've learned by man made religion principles according to handling circumstances in my own way and method. Not going to God directly for all things. I never wanted to endure anything, and that's why I said the wrong words to you guys (and they both laughed). She continued; "Instead of endurance, I just came up with my own solutions for the problems that I faced. Rebecca said "You know that is the backbone for every so called Religion in this world" and she agreed and said "You're right. Rebecca continued.. " I learned that people have changed the motto from what is humanly acceptable to what they think should be acceptable. Instead of trusting God they have promoted fear and methods for the things they hate to see happen. Not sitting back and saying, God has a reason for this, a bigger plan that we have to trust Him to fix, and relying on His work to be fulfilled in us that only He can do. They have mixed cultural beliefs and made it a form of religion and practices that they think are good enough for God. But God doesn't see the outside of a person, (seeing that we all must physically die) He looks at the heart. The heart of man. "That's right!" Misses Cakes exclaimed. She goes on "We can never be accepted by tradition customs and practices, but only by God's grace ... "As her mom comes out and interrupts her, Rebecca said "Oh Miss Cakes, I gotta go! my mom wants to know what happened." She replied "Okay well talk some more tomorrow, I understand and you can call me Natalie." She said "Okay, Natalie God Bless you and talk soon." And they ended.

So Rebecca went in the house with her mom to finally explain what had happened. Her mom turned off the t.v and sat her down. She said "Now, I can tell you've been through alot seeing that there's dirt all over your shirt and your face looks a little different, plus your hair is all over the place and you took long ... Now I hope you haven't been out doing bad business with that girl Ashley, please say it aint so!" Rebecca was about to respond and her mom interrupted and said "I know, I know you're grown and you know how to handle things but I just know how clever that Ashley is. And you've changed, you've changed so much Rebecca, I wouldn't want you falling into your old habbits again, You've grown for the better and I support you all of the way! Ashley is, ... "Rebecca said "Wait, mom! I just wanna stay off of the subject of Ashley for just one minute, in fact I don't even think this is her story in the first place but she got alot of role!." "I met this beautiful woman on the inside and out that really touched my heart and inspired me to be more like you and I understand that most times I've been a pest to you by going out so much and doing so many of the wrong things. I've been in the way of my own self and life and yours too, and it's only now that I see this, but this woman has taught me so much value in us denying ourselves to follow Jesus as mankind in general. Not just for our own personal purposes but for Our Creator! The GREAT I AM! He is the one that influences us to do good mom … It's not in our own selves that we can do good. And He's the one that structures our life to go according that His purpose be fufilled. I learned that just by an Angel that I came across 3 different times in my life. Her mom said "O yea, and what's her name?" She said "Natalie." Her name is Natalie mom and she doesn't deserve the credit, only God does! But I tell you she is a precious work of art by God Himself!. "Honey, so are you" Her mom said. "Yes mom I know, thank you. But I do know that this woman has truly given me deep understanding on how to live and be just by living out her life. And you, you have given me insight to that too!" So Rebecca's mom said "That's great honey and I'm so glad to hear all of these things." "Is my car okay? have you gotten the groceries?"

Rebecca said, "Yes mom I've gotten the groceries … But I don't know if the ice cream is still alive" *As she laughs.* Then she says as she's walking to go get the groceries "You know mom, maybe oneday we should take a picnic at the beach and just relax and talk some more." "Maybe we should Rebecca, that sounds like a good idea." Okay when do you wanna go? Cause I'm free whenever, and I'm all ears and ready to hear ya" said her mom.. Rebecca said, well you know I'm free and ready to go when you are too. and they laughed and kept talking while bringing the groceries in. "Tomorrow, I wanna go to a friend's wedding." Her mom said, "A wedding?! tomorrow so soon?" Who's wedding is it? And Rebecca said "Well, it's my friend Natalie." Her mom said "Natalie … Natalie that you were just telling me about?" Rebecca said "Why, yes it's her and she invited me. … and you could come too I guess, if you wanna come … " "Oh what a nice way of inviting me" her mom said. She said "Yes I'm sorry mom but this was a last minute deal." "I understand honey." She said. So she asked her "Well what are you gonna wear?" and she said she thought about it, and was just gonna come home and decide what to wear from one of her dresses she had. Her mom offered her one of her dresses and she jokingly insisited that that wouldn't be necessary. Later on she looked through her wardrobe and found a few things she could wear, remembering that Natalie introduced a pair of her baby pink heels to Rebecca to go along with her white dress she decided on the white and pink. She had an all white dress with a pink pearled necklace and sheer cover up. Her clutch was small and baby pink too with a shade of white on it.

The next day, most of the guests were there before Rebecca arrived, (though she thought she was coming early.) She came by herself and drove her mom's van to the place where the wedding was (It was outside). And she parked and got out. As she walked, the place was so fancy and beautiful and she was looking for a place to sit down because she wasn't used to high heels when Natalie saw her and came up to her with the shoes. So she ran to the bathroom to trade. She got finished and came back out and saw Natalie waiting there for her. She asked her "Why are you here? aren't you supposed to be still getting ready?" She said "Yea, I'm okay I was coming to make sure you were alright." She said "Yes girl, I am perfectly fine, go and enjoy your wedding you still have to prepare, Is there anything you need assistance with?" She said "Well ... Come with me upstairs and yes I do need some help." So they took off upstairs until Rebecca said "Wait hold on I can't go that fast, these heels are in the way!" "And Natalie said, "Oh come on, you can go a little faster than that can't you? Just try to push your way up these stairs girl you can make it." She was taunting and playing with her.. So Rebecca said "Okay, I see your game.. I'll try.." and then when they reached the room, they went inside this big huge makeup room where she had people doing make up and hair for her and her bridesmades. They got all dolled up and Natalie showed her quick ways of doing eye brow makeup that she never knew and no one ever taught her. She said, wow Natalie, how do you know these things? and she replied "Don't you even know?" God taught me these things. He is merciful to us as His creation and understands us very well. He even stretches out His hand as far as to our little independent things. Though He tries to pull us away from things of the flesh, He allows us access to use these things." Rebecca said "Even makeup?" So Natalie insisted, She said "God doesn't care about these little things, think about it Becc, We use our computers and technology for the goodness of The Lord and those are some of the worse things that is not even His own system, though we know that everything is His. Remember Paul says using these things as not abusing them, for the fashion of this world passeth away? O Yea! Rebecca said.

So Natalie continues ... Yes, we have access to these things to get the Word of God out! and He is showing how these things mean nothing to an Almighty God because He is sitting back on His throne in His Glory waiting for His children to praise Him in Spirit and in Truth! Not in the letter, not law bidden, but with our hearts closely knit to Him! She goes on to say, "We have to know what sin is, and what mercy our Father has for us!" If we abuse His mercy then we are not claiming ourselves to be His children. So we must understand what He wants and what is acceptable to Him according to our lives, He tells us that flesh and blood will not inherit the Kingdom." And He tells us that no man can please God in the flesh and that Faith pleases Him. Faith is not a feeling, Faith is a trusting in God and His promises. He says "If you live by the law, you will die." Therefore there is nothing else we can do by the works of the flesh. It is written Becc." and she was finished ; So by that time, Rebecca was indeed completely dolled up and she looked beautiful. So Rebecca asked her, "What about you? don't you still have to get ready? It is your wedding you know?" And she said to her "Yes, I know, I'm gonna get ready but I wanted to make sure my bridesmades and you were ready first. My time is coming Becc, and so is yours. So Rebecca said "What do you mean?" And Natalie replied her "I think you know.." so she just shook her head and they both laughed. She said you know Natalie, no one calls me Becc for short, and I love that name. She said "Oh I'm sorry, I didn't even ask you if it was okay for me to call you that." "She said no, no I really love that name and you were the one to think of calling me it which is no coincidence." She said.. "I thank God for you Nat, even though I know we haven't known eachother long it feels like we've known eachother forever to be honest."

She responded "The feeling is mutual indeed Becc, and you know, that's what happens when 2 are on the same road." God says, how can two walk together except they agreed." and that hit home for her and Ashley's walk. She understood how her and Ashley kept disagreeing and split because they were on different roads. She understood perfectly how everything was spiritual and it just made her want to know God more. And that's what Rebecca liked about Natalie, Natalie made her want to know God more. So Rebecca left for Natalie to get dressed up. She went down stairs into this inner room where the decorations and food was and she spotted the cake on a table and walked over to look at it. On the cake said, "The story of Mrs. Natalie and Kevin" And she blushed for her friend. She was so happy that God's precious Angel could find a good man like that & she knew how her and Ashley were wrong with Kevin when he delivered them pizza; and how bad she felt playing games with him and she said "Kevin really does deserve her." Natalie decides to run up behind her to startle her Rebecca said "Oh yeah, well 2 can play that game, and she pretended as if she was going to jump on the cake, so Natalie laughed and said, You know Becc, God wants all these things we want for us; just not the bad crazy stuff. and teaches us lessons throughout our lives." and Becc said "Yea that is true ... You mean like the thrills of life? the high's and lows are like the roller coaster rides we try to enjoy?" "Yes exactly, you got it." She goes on.. "I really believe that God is teaching us something about dancing in the rain."

(SCRIPTURE Phil 4:4) tells us how we Glory in tribulations. Rebecca agreed. We seek thrills in this life that are temporary to pleasing the flesh, so when the ones that God has prepared for us to climb over, our minds should be elevated to where we will recieve it as a thrill and not as a headache. We have to conquer all these things and give God thanks in knowing that this life is not all He has in store" That is the roller coaster of life we are on ... So Becca agreed much and said, Wow, you look so pretty Natalie!" "And so do you Becc" She responded.

They went on together to the ceremony and Rebecca said "Wow this sure is the best wedding I've been to." It's not common or traditional like the usual. You really put a spin on this and just have fully submitted yourself to cherish and spend time with your guests, to make sure we are well taken care of Natalie, and who knew such an Angel like you would treat her guests so well. (Natalie laughed) as Rebecca continued ... "I'm not saying that to be funny, But God really has Blessed you." And she said "And I can't take the credit for it, it is truly the grace I've found Rebecca, just like you did" He showers each one of us with His love so much that we have no choice but to give our lives to Him and give Him All The Glory. We gotta know and realize who we are and that we are nothing, and can do nothing compared to what He's done. He just wants us to hold out, and jump through every obstacle, knowing that they are not really obstacles because we've already overcome through His name, and are walking in His footsteps. He has already made the path for us to walk on ... (They were almost there, & the park where the ceremony was held was really big. When she said ...)" You know how your natural parents used to tell you that you can play, after you do something?" Yes, Rebecca responded.. She goes on, "Well after we (as God's children,) finish spending our time with Him, then He allows us to go and play. It is like the same way. He just wants our time, not even to do anything sometimes but to just be still and listen to Him knowing that He is God alone." Wow, Amen" Rebecca said. "He taught me that too when I was going through a withdrawl from seperating with Ashley." Natalie told her "I know, I know … And that is why He wants to wing you off of the things you've learned and old habbits you've picked up from that relationship. He wants you to completely be All His and wants to teach us in His new way." "Yea, Amen" said Rebecca.

The two finally made it to the ceremony when Natalie had to go away, and Rebecca went to sit down. Everyone was there and seated and the music was playing for the bride to come down. The weather was beautiful, it was warm with a nice slight breeze every now and again and sunny. The decorations were white and pink..And black. Her husband to be wore a black suit with white and black bow tie (It was sharp.) Rebecca's bridesmaids wore pink pearlish dresses and white pearls for accessories. In such a short period of time, there stood alot of guests. It wasn't your typical wedding, there were alot of twists and cool stuff that happened in which no one would expect. There was alot of food and drinks for everyone. And Kevin "Bigshot's" Dad was there. Natalie wasn't the one to try and make the wedding fancy, she didn't mind everything being simple and that is why when asked about her "color scheme" for the wedding, her first thought was simply "Pink and White". A common color, she didn't want any hassle and they found the place with a breeze.

She didn't want anyone to loose thier hat. Or nothing complicated for anyone to loose sleep over. But she got spoiled anyway and The

Lord Blessed her even still. At the end when Natalie through her bouquet, you probably guessed it ... Yep, Rebecca was the one to catch it! And she told Rebecca," this is not the end of the world, not even a new start for me.. I've learned so much and come so far that I believe The Lord saw it fit for me to hand over my authority to my husband." And then she played with her to scare her ... "You do know that once you get married, you have to hand over all of your authority to your husband right?" and Rebecca knew she was playing so she squinted her face at her as she went on.. "Yea, it's funny but it is true in a way." But God made marriage to be a good thing. It is the heart of man that corrupts what is good to turn it into other things. And we know that we don't live for this flesh and how other people see us. And we know that God says in His Word "Flesh and Blood will not inherit the Kingdom." So while we make the little things down here so important, God is constantly trying to get our attention on Heavenly things that don't relate to the flesh or carnality.

At that point, Rebecca was highly influenced and elevated. She appreciated her friend Natalie so much that she just praised God and danced as she dropped the bouqet. Through The Holy Spirit of God, Natalie was taking her places that she had never been been before and she was loving every bit of it!" So afterwards, everyone went to the room where the cake was to sing and to dance. People got introduced, and Rebecca got introduced to Kevin's Dad and he told her things about the business they owned and how they were able to prepare for the wedding in such a short time. They talked, laughed and danced. They ate and had a good time. While Ashley was imprisoned, she spent her time in there trying to figure out how to do more wickedly. There was a Bible there for her, especially for her that wasn't there by coincidence. For her to read, but she didn't want to pay attention to what God was trying to show her. She was younger in her late twenty's so they didn't want to put her with any inmates in her room. She was just left alone, which was good, but she didn't want to heed to the opportunity to come to know The Lord.

In the end of it all, Ashley was in jail for a matter of a few weeks then they placed her on probation; so she didn't really get a chance to have that one on one time with God. Instead of motivation to do good, Ashley was even more motivated to get into mischief once her probation period was over. So 3 weeks went by when she was released and by this time, she had gotten off of her probation. After sweet talking her way out of every situation, lying and decieving people, she went back to her old ways and started causing trouble again. Until oneday when she went out of her house to do mischief, she came to this park where there were 2 young women around the age of 20 sitting down talking. So she passed them, and when she passed them by she had a soda bottle so she sneakingly splashed out her soda on one of the young women's dress to pretend it was an accident and she said "oh I'm sorry" while the girl gasped because it was cold. The girl was mad and didn't want an apology but still said, "It's okay, it's fine" as she waited for Ashley to go away. So Ashley kept walking until she spotted a bee hive. So she took it down with a stick and tried to put it inside of a bush near where the young women were sitting down. She placed it behind them where they were sitting and hid behind the bush so she began to shake it so that the bees would come out. She was acting like a child and refused to try to get to understand Spiritual things. So eventually the bees did come out of the hive and gravitate towards where the two ladies were sitting and they liked the smell of soda on they young lady's leg that didn't completley come off. So the bee stung her. They both got up and was introduced to more meddling with Ashley when she, Took off her sandals and began swatting around as if the bees were attacking her too. She was pretend screaming and swinging her shoe around when all of a sudden, she came close to the other girl and slapped her across the face with the shoe and said … "O wow ma'am I'm so sorry, these bees were attacking me." The young woman with a hurt face just stopped and didn't know what to say or do at that point. She just held the side of her face where Ashley hit in hurt and said "It is okay … There seems to be alot of trouble in this little area of the park so were leaving." and Ashley said "Yea, I get ya; well where are you going?" They thought it was kind of strange that she tried to get to know them after those 2 incidents but they didn't pay it any mind. So one of the girls spoke and said, soon, we'll be leaving to go home. So Ashley said, well why go home on a day like this where it's so pretty outside, we should look for something to do. And the girls looked at eachother and just shook their head at Ashley. So Ashley continued.. Don't you know there are people out here in need of attention and things that need to be done? They said well, yea..

She stopped them and said.. "Right, so why spend all of our time here at a park just sitting and doing nothing?" "My name is Ashley by the way, what's you guy's name?" So the women introduced themselves as Stacey and Monique. (Stacey was the one that got the soda poured out on her dress and stung by a bee, but Monique got slapped in the face with the shoe.) She said "here let me save your numbers." You know it's a small world and girls need to stick together, don't you agree?" and they both were easily influenced and said yes, but … So Ashley interrupted again and said, "Besides, there is way too much fun out here in this life to be bored." "I got an idea, when was the last time you two ever been out on a date?" Monique said "Well the last time I went, I barely knew the guy but he offered me a ride and I just decided to go with him." So Ashley said "So that's perfect, he was probably a good guy, and we should meet more good guys like that." But Monique continued and said "Well, no actually he raped me and took my jewelry then told me that if I ever told anyone about it, he would kill me. but that was when I was 15." So Ashley said "How old are you?" And Monique replied "I'm 21 now". So Ashley said wow that was 6 years ago, girl you are long overdue for a good time.. and this time he won't be the one doing the raping, we should get into guys heads."

So Stacey didn't like the idea and stopped her. She said "Wait a minute, what kind of sick ideas are you thinking of for us to do "have fun"? But Ashley said "Sick?" No, no no honey, I was only suggesting that this was the wrong thing for that young man to do. Calm down and relax Stacey. I was only saying that the guy that did that to her was very inconsiderate of her feelings. So I suggest that WE, meaning us 3, go and show these people how we can work as a team together to do more for eachother." Ashley went on and said "Stacey, how long have you and Monique known eachother?" And she said "More than 5 years. Why?" And Ashley began and said "Oh wow really that's a long time, so where were you when your friend got raped? I'm sure you went out of your way to help her." But Stacey couldn't answer the question because she felt bad. Stacey was the one that told her she should go when Monique was feeling uncomfortable about the situation and asked her." So the 2 started having inquires about their friendship when Ashley spoke out again and said "Did you know that you can save a whole Village just by being part of helping people out in small ways, like even just by talking to them?" (Though Ashley was not concerned about saving any villages, she wanted to see where Stacey's mind was.) So Stacey said "Really? Wow I didn't think of it like that." (In trying to get over the topic of Monique's situation.) She continued and said "Well, yea maybe we should get together and hang out at my place I can have you guys over and we can play cards." Ashley said "Cards?" "And what's up with you 2 girls dresses? Don't you wanna put on something more thrilling?"

and Stacey replied "Well it's Easter Sunday and ... " And Ashley interrupted her and said "Yea, yea yea, I get it Easter ... " She said "Well, I'm more comfortable with nothing on, that's how I prefer to look but some religous people might judge me." So the girls didn't say anything much and they continued on the way to Stacey's house as Ashley kept upholding the conversation.

So as time went on, the 3 women became closer and closer. Stacey always had her question marks up about Ashley but she never said much after that incident. Monique thought that Ashley was fun so she just used her for the ride to get to know more people and have a good time. So oneday, when Ashley was on her way to her new friend Monique's house. She had plans to seperate the 2 seeing that Stacey had to many concerns against Ashley she felt that it was hurting her agendas. So she was going to catch the bus to her friends house and right after she left out, she heard some noise from down the street, but she didn't pay much attention to it and she just went to walk up to her bus stop. As time went on and the bus prolonged, she heard a voice say "Hey pretty young lady, got a minute?" and she turned around to see who it was and it was the guy that followed her home and teased her after her and Rebecca left that club oneday. So she knew it was him and recognized the car and was scared. She pretended as if she didn't recognize him and said. "No I'm sorry, my bus is coming soon." So he drove up closely to her and she just stood there then he said "Don't you know who I am pretty lady?" and she said, nope I don't know who you are but I can't talk right now." So the guy got out of the car and Ashley backed away from the bus stop and started walking away from him. But he just kept his car parked and followed after her as she picked up the pace. She said what do you want? I don't have anything that belongs to you do I?" as she's walking fast with him walking fast behind her.

And he says to her "Yea you do, you have my heart and it belongs to me.. I want it back." So Ashley said "There is nothing I can do about that." There was no one there to help her and nothing she could do as she came to a dead end street. She started too look on each side and no one was around there were just empty houses. She hoped that someone would pull up in their drive way but no one was there to save her. So the guy just kept getting closer and closer till they ended up in someones backyard. And she yelled "I'm sorry!" She also said a curse word. But she stooped down on her knees to the ground in someone's backyard and said, whatever I did look dude, I'm sorry just leave me alone cause I gotta make it to my friends house. In fact if you don't mind could you take me there please, and I'll give you whatever you want." But this guys eye was evil and set on doing her harm. He didn't know why he wanted to harm her but he just did. He was being used by the enemy to repay Ashley for all she did. She was granted mercy several times throughout her life and she refused to accept the call placed on her life to follow what was good but instead she wanted to do evil. Well, the guy did end up having his way with her. He did some things that don't need to be named or mentioned which unfortunately left Ashley hurt and confused and damaged her pride. She didn't want to go out anymore and she ended up having to go to the hospital. She lost her new friends that she made and many other things happened during the course of her life as she got older. She got impregnated by that man, and had a child to take care of now. This was her Blessing that she recieved even after all of the things that she did, God still wanted to fill in her gap between Him and her. This innocent child who did nothing wrong, even though it wasn't by her submission, would help her; but she ended up leaving the baby (while she was a new born,) at a train station near her house. And she eventually left the house and found a job. She moved up to become a supervisor at her job and took over people and severly misusing and mistreating them.

She helped her company move up by her wicked schemes and ways, and eventually became CEO of her company. They started to love Ashley so much and began advancing her very fast. They admired and wanted to be like her. She would boss people around and treat them unfairly. Those that wanted to do good, she would push around and try to get them to do things against their nature to make them feel uncomfortable. Since she didn't give her life to God, she only grew worse and worse as a person. She got many offers in big businesses and forced her way to be the top cheif of the company so that no one could boss her around. But everyone saw her as a beautiful sincere smart woman who only had a small personality issue they found her quirky and fun, someone to spice up the job and it's ridicule. Ashley made people feel bad all the time telling them "My sin isn't bigger than yours" and so men saw her as an easy to change situation and all that she needed was something that they could give, TLC; They challenged themselves to try and win her heart and to change her, but what they didn't see was that for God to do a work on her, He would have to undue years of damage and she would have to submit to this work. And Ashley was unwilling to change no matter what came her way. Ashley was reaching a point of no return and the sufferings of all of her victims; They would find peace in God's sight. He doesn't strive with men for long so at some point, if a person is not willing to be covered by His mercy, they already have chosen their own destiny. But God's hand stretches out so far still. Her time wasn't up because she was still alive, yet she did so much evil and would not repent. Oneday, she was sitting in her office when she remembered the words of the little boy at the park that told her to repent. The one that she couldn't get to and she wanted to know why she could get to those girls but for some reason she just couldn't get to that little boy and his mother. So they held on in her memory for so long until she finally decided to do something about people who made her feel like she didn't have any advantage over them. She started going against Christians. She started to make so much money and still hated her life and took it out on the people around her. She thought that if she could be rich, then she would be happy. But it just made her more unhappy.

So eventually she ran into this company called "The Square Garden Inn" that was so prosperous through standing on it's Christian values, and she wanted to take over the company. Not knowing the owner of that company, she made a proposal to take over the company's family owned business, but got denied several times. So she wondered why she couldn't get the owner to submit to her proposal; seeing that she could easily persuade anybody she wanted. She went on a search for the owner of the business personally. Somehow she knew, that if she could just talk to him one on one instead of on a computer screen, then she could trick him into getting him to hand over the business. And so she decided to try and take him out on a date oneday to sit him down and talk to him; Oneday she would try to trick him into meeting up with him and charm him. So she carefully planned out the scheme and even had other people in on it to take him down. Oneday he was walking out from the gate of his mansion with his exercise clothes on. He was going to jog around the area; and she saw him, but she saw Kevin too, then Natalie. So she was suprised to see them there! And She thought "What in the world could they be doing here in this mansion?"

So as she tried to figure it out in her mind (forgetting that Kevin mentioned anything about his fathers business,) He then ran up close to the gates of the mansion to jog out, and so she got scared thinking he would see her and backed away (She was in near a tall tree.) He didn't see her and he just started to jog along this long pathway that went around the huge mansion and into a park. So he ran. After a little while, Ashley decided to drive to the park where he ran instead. So she got there and stepped out of the vehicle she was driving, in her red tight fitting "news reporter looking" blazer and skirt, she came out and walked. She had on black heels, her black bangs with a long, thick, gold streaked curly wig full of hair. She had bright red lipstick on as well. She walked out and onto the grass, adjusting her sunglasses she switches over to him as he's jogging. She stopped him and started conversing with him while he took a breath. She told him that she just spotted him running and wanted to get to know him better. She was attracted to the way he ran and thought that the sweat coming off of his muscles reflecting from the sunlight is what attracted her to him. She insisted that they go out on at least one date so he could see what type of person she was, but he was just eager to finish his course in running that he quickly agreed "Yes, sure" to hurry up and get the conversation over with. So she agreed that they should go out on this "date" and she gave him her number and made sure to take his then he continued on his run.

So now she had all this to think about (the fact that she saw Kevin and Natalie in that mansion and what it could mean.) That disturbed her and she hoped it wouldn't interfere in the game that she was trying to play. She sat down and figured it out. She came up with a plan that if she could just get him intoxicated to make him sign some business papers, then she would own his business in no time. Rebecca and her mom did end up moving close to Natalie and Kevin and began to do business with his Dad. So Rebecca was with Kevin oneday and asked him "What color would your Dad like on the layout of his new logo for the company. I won't ask him because what I'm building, well lets just say I want the whole thing to be a suprise. But if it came out pink and purple I'm sure instead of suprised he would be mad. I just wanna have an idea of where to start." So he said, well good ol' blue never hurt anybody Becc, just don't go doing any green or gray that would be kind of off ya know.. haha ... Navy Blue would be perfect!" So she said Okay. She headed off to the library to get some papers done when Natalie ran up behind her to suprise her and said "I wanna walk with you, let's go ... " So they walked and talked until they got close to the library and Natalie said "Ooh wait, let's stop in here to get some eats first pleeeeeaase? I'm hungry." So they went inside this small restaurant where they were able to get burgers and fries but it was a semi-fancy restaurant with not a whole lot of people. Pretty relaxed and reserved.

As they were sitting down and waiting for their food, Rebecca spotted Natalie's Dad sitting by himself at a table, as Natalie was on the opposite side of them, she said "Dad?" as she squinted her eyes at him making sure she wasn't seeing things. So Natalie turned around saw him then turned back to Rebecca saying "I wonder what my Dad is doing here, I'll go check on him, wait here at the table Becc, for the food; Brb. So she went to go sit down and talk to him and as Ashley was coming out from the bathroom she saw Natalie sitting down at the table and ran back in the bathroom mad and frustrated. She thought "I should've known she would somehow get in the way of this when I saw her and Kevin. I've gotta get rid of her. So Natalie and her Dad kept talking and she asked him ... "What are you doing here Dad? Are you all alone here by yourself?" And he insisted, "No, I'm just here with a hot date! She's a pretty little lady she went to the bathroom and should be out shortly, I want you to meet her." So he then asked her "What are you doing here?" So she replied "Well, I have Becc here with me at the table and we just went to grab a burger and fries before heading off to get some work done." He said "Oh I see. Well, hang around here she should be out here shortly if you don't mind." and she said, sure. Our food should be coming out shortly so I don't mind." And the two kept talking while waiting for her to come out of the bathroom.

Ashley in the bathroom thought to herself "Man, she's still there! now what am I gonna do?" So she grabbed her phone to call him and he said "Oh look, that's her now, I hope she's not in any trouble" and picked up the phone. She said "Hey you, I ran into a bit of a mess, do you mind helping me please? Oh, and are you still by yourself at the table?" So he answered, "OOooh, oh, well actually no, let me come there I'm sorry just hold on a minute and I'll be right there." So he left Natalie at the table telling her to wait there a minute and went to the bathroom to see what was wrong. When he got there (By that time, Ashley had splashed water all on herself and smeared her makeup to make it seem as though an accident had occured. So when he saw her he said "Wow, what's wrong? What happened to you?" She said, "Shh, shh I know I don't want anyone to see me like this." and he said "Well, okay. My daughter's here and was just at the table wanting to meet you but I'll call her and tell her to hold off this time and well meet her some other time." So he picked up the phone and called her.

She answered and said "Dad, is everything okay?" And he answered her "Yes sweetie, everything is fine, but look hang on in meeting my date. were gonna see you next time on, we kind of need some more time alone, me and my date." So Natalie was really questionable as to what had happened but she said "(sighs) Okay Dad, no problem well see you guys soon." So he hung up and said "What are we gonna do now?" While Ashley said "Here, let me cover my face with this binder and well walk out ... I'm sure the restaurant wouldn't mind us using it for an emergency." So she took this white binder that was sitting near the bathroom, next to the main entrance and covered the side of her face as she walked out with him leaving the table and their food. And once they got out, she realized she left her purse so she asked him if he would go back in and get her purse for her, so he did; and as he passed back by Rebecca and Natalie he said "Hey Becc how's it going?" and she greeted him, then he said "Look guys, I'm really sorry things are like this, something unfortunate happened to my date and she just didn't want to be seen to be embarrassed." He continued, "I'm really sorry guys.." So they both said, "That's okay Dad." Natalie said "It's no bigg, we understand just enjoy the rest of your day and well see you later on okay?" She kissed him on the cheek. He said "Thank you my sweet daughter I always wanted. And he took off to get her purse and he headed out."

Ashley looked down to the ground and back up to him with an imputent face and said "I'm so sorry the date turned out this way." As they were walking her still dripping wet with a wet face smeared with makeup. And he said to her "Things happen, that's quite alright, but what exactly did happen?" So she said "Oh, well.. you see.. and then she dropped her phone to the ground and made a scene. She said "Oh nooo, I hope it didn't break! and then she pressed a button to make it ring and pretended to pick it up and said "Hello?" And then started talking to herself on the phone. So she told him to hold on a min. and she went to the side and kept talking. By then, he was a little frustrated and just rolled his eyes and said ok. He thought to himself "This girl seems to have a lot with her." But he payed it no more mind and stood there and waited until she got off the phone. So Ashley kept talking to herself as she was thinking of a plan of what to tell him and what to do to get him back on a date. Once she got off of the phone she went back up to him and apologized. Then she said "You know what, I have a better idea that we should've done before. Let's go to my house and that way I can get cleaned up then we can talk a little more privately, how does that sound?" He was a little nervous and embarrassed and said "Oh oh sure, that sounds fine. Okay … " So they got back to the car and went to her house. It was about a 15 minute drive as they pulled up into her driveway, he saw that her place was really nice and said to her "Wow, this really is a nice place. how long have you been here?" She said "Oh that's nothing, wait until you see the inside. This place has been my dream home for roughly 5 years now." So he said "Wow, this is really nice!" As he glanced all around at the beautiful decor outside of the house. She said "Ya coming in?"

So the two stepped out into the house and once they got in he noticed all of the awards she had and the pictures that were on the wall. And said to her "What do you do that you have won so many awards? Are these all yours?" And she said "Well, yes … I'm the head C.E.O of my company but … that's neither here nor there, would you like me to get you a glass of wine." He said "Sure, oh and would you mind a cup of water please too? My throat seems to be a little bit dry." She said "That's okay, I could get you a cup of water, sure." So as she went, He just kept on gazing at the pictures on the wall when he spotted a picture of what looked like Rebecca. So he said "Hmmm.. this sure does look like Becc." Then she came back towards him after setting the drinks down on the table and said "Would you mind, I can take your blazer for you." So he said "Sure" taking off the blazer, he asked her "Who is this little girl in this picture?" She sure does look alot like my daughter in laws friend Rebecca. So she gasped within herself saying in her head "Rebecca, he knows Rebecca? Natalie's FRIEND still??!" And she didn't know what to say to him so she said "Oh her, that's one of my old friends from school, do you mind having homeade lasagna to eat?" and he said (As he wouldn't take his eyes off of the picture) "Oh sure, I don't mind, then he said by the way what is her name?" So Ashley fumbles all around thinking of what to tell him and she lies to him yelling out "Stacey". And he just kept starring at her in the picture, and thinking "This just has to be Rebecca, or her twin and I don't know that Rebecca even has a twin." So he just shrugged his shoulders and said "Oh well." He ended up going to the table a little confused and Ashley turned on some jazz music to relax him and said "Take it easy and unwind, mi casa es su casa. Then she rubbed his shoulders handing him his glass of wine.

She quickly switched to another topic and they started talking about traveling and the different places each of them had been. He told her that he's been to China once and to Africa twice. And he told her different things about China and how developed the infrastructure was. He went on to tell her about the quality and how they spent their time making there products to the best of it's possible potential and that is why here in America we see many of there products here being bought and sold so easily and at a fast pace. He told her about how China was one of the Countries that were far away from God, yet they had so many advancements and he went on to explain to her why when she cut him off and started to talk about other things. (She didn't want to talk about The Lord and didn't know Him, so it made her feel uncomfortable.) She kept encouraging him to drink his wine and she went to the kitchen asking if he wanted some crackers and cheese until the lasagna was ready. He said No, and she came back out with the bottle of wine then sat down at the table with him. So he drank his first bottle of wine and then he asked her "What exactly is it that you liked about me when you saw me running outside again?" And she giggled and said "Well, for starters I saw your huge muscles dripping with sweat as they glissened from the sunlight. And when you ran, I started gazing into your brow bone and how determined and concentrated you were and it made me feel a little excited." So he said "Well, I guess I do have that effect on people from time to time when I run." and she took that and ran with it. She went on and poured him another glass of wine then said "Well, you know what they say "Men are like fine wine, they take time to mature." And then she laughed.

After her knowing that he knew Rebecca, she wanted to get as much information out of him as possible and he was an honest man that had nothing to hide. So she asked him saying "You know, I noticed something about you … You do stand true to your principles of your faith, that is quality and all women want that. What makes you so sure and grounded on what you believe?" He said "Well, one thing I know is that God has His way of showing us things He wants us to understand and we have our way of communicating to Him." He goes on.. "The most effective way we can communicate to God is by giving Him our heart and undivided attention, that is our recognition of who He is. In the scripture my daughter in law reads to me every now and again, what a sweet heart; it says "Be still and know that I am God." So she said "Hmm, well that is interesting … And what makes you so confident as an entrepenuer? Is it your faith?" And he quickly answered "Absolutely!" "We stand 100 percent on what we know and believe. Our faith is the absolute foundation for our company's prosperity.

That is the root of why we have even been prosperous thus far." So she was amused and smiled then said "Hmmm.." within herself. She knew a little bit of the Bible and what it says about sin so she thought it would be fun to catch him in his confidence as he continued speaking. She said "O well that's great …) She didn't want to fully condemn him yet because she hadn't yet gotten the information she was seeking out of him, and she didn't get him to sign the papers yet either. "You know, I'm so sorry I wasn't able to meet your daughter? You said it was?" He said "Yes, I call her my daughter because she's like a daughter to me but she's actually

my daughter in law. Her name is Natalie, she's like an Angel."
She said, "Yes, I remember her name, you told me already." So he
continued "Yes well hopefully there will be other times we spend
together and you will get a chance to meet her. So she agreed and
said yes. She asked him if his "daughter" had any close friends
or if she was just a loner" as he finished his 2nd cup of wine. She
was ready to pour him another. Then he said "Well, yea she's got
Becc." And Ashley gasped.

"Becc, you say?" She said to him as she inches over sitting on
the table next to his seat. And he was feeling kind of warm and
loosened his tie then said "Yes, Rebecca ... " He went on to
say "Rebecca's an Angel too. We met her when she was going
through alot and had just came out of an issue with one of her old
friends that she grew up with. But she found The Lord and her
and Natalie remained friends ever since. This was about 5 years
ago." She said "Hmmm, you don't say?" He said "Yes. But this
was all God's ordained plan, I believe. I needed Becca so much.
She has been such an inspiration, help and asset in the business
and that is why I know this was not by coincidence that we met,
and everything worked out very well for all of our good." So she
glanced down at him and just smiled and shook her head agreeing
with him." She said "Oh I think the lasagna's ready, let me go
check, I'll be right back. As she made sure to rub him on his
shoulder by her hip then she switched her hips to walk towards
the kitchen."

When she came back, she offered him another glass of wine, but
by then he was finished and she asked him if he wanted to take a
tour of her house, so he said "Sure." So they went walking around
the house (It was big) and she began showing him all of her
different rooms and in one of her rooms, there was a drawer where
some of her collectibles and she pulled it out and showed him

some collectible baseball cards, comic books, and magazines she wanted to get rid of so she asked him "Do you know of anywhere I could donate these old things?" Pretending to be charitable, she went on … "I have so many things to offer and when I see the less fortunate I think, who are we to just hold on to so many things when there are people out here who have never had things like this that we look at and want to just throw away. They only wish to have things like that." So he agreed with her and said "That is true!" We should always give to the less fortunate; Especially when we have more than enough." He answered her and said "I don't know of any place to donate collectible items but I'm sure it would be easy to find." and she said "Yea, it should be easy" then she closed the drawer and they continued the tour of that room.

This room was big in size and had an Ultra King sized bed with a canopy. So she took him around the room (it had a lot of distance) and she made him sit on the bed and test it out to see if it was comfy. Then she began talking about the bed and how she found it. She said "This bed was a once in a lifetime thing for me to find because of it's size. I wanted a room for guests where the bed would be extra gigantic and the guests would feel nice and comfy for the times they visited and slept." So he laid down on it and said whoa well what a great idea!" She assured him that it was okay to relax on the bed. And he did, and the bed was comfortable and to his liking. The bed was 12 feet long and rare to find. *It was the kind of bed that was hard to get off of because once you got on it, it would put you to sleep.* So she laid down and stretched out alongside him and continued to talk. She made up things about herself as a child, telling him what type of girl she used to be before she became a big company owner. And how she used to be such a goodie two shoes and never minded the people around her that would cause trouble but always tried her best to do what was good. And he thought to himself "This is such a nice woman, I'm afraid that if I'm around her for too long, she might get me to marry her as he smirked." She kept talking and she said "Mr. Dean, have you ever been married before?" He said "Why yes, yes I have. I got married when I was in my late 30's to a very special woman and had my son. My son's name is Kevin." She said "I know ... "He said "You do? how do you know Kevin?" But she corrected herself seeing she made that mistake and said "What I meant was, I know you probably missed your first wife." and he said "Well, yes I do, I miss her every second but she was taken away early from us due to a bad situation that I would prefer not to name." She then said "Oh I'm very sorry.." He said it was okay and that He didn't mind talking about her, he just didn't like bringing up the situation of what happened. So she changed the subject and they both got up off of the bed and continued to tour the rest of the house.

By the time the tour had ended, it had taken them about 2 hours and she realized that the lasagna was still in the oven and they heard a "beep, beep," Beeping noise. They were in her room and she said "Oh the lasagna, I have to go downstairs, wait here ... "And she rushed downstairs to get the lasagna out of the oven and it was well done. So he stood in the room gazing at the decor and he started thinking about that picture again and if he could just see it one more time and ask Rebecca about it. Or maybe somehow get a picture of it through his phone. He started feeling woozy and tipsy a little (*after deciding to have one more glass of wine.*) And he didn't like the feeling he was getting but he ignored it until she came back upstairs. She came upstairs to him and said "Woo I see someone's feeling a little relaxed." As she walks over to him with a smile. (By this time, he was leaning on the bed rail feeling a little different.) She attempted to mistakenly sit on his lap and said "Oops" as she slided herself onto the bed next to where he was.

She was being very repulsive and ready to take advantage of him to make him sign the papers at this point (*because he started acting like he couldn't control himself.*) So she pressed on with the agenda and got close to him and asked him "How do you feel?" and he said to her "Well, to be honest Ashley I think I feel like I wanna go back downstairs. I'm getting a little hot." So she was insulted and said "Fine, let's go then since you're not comfortable. And he said "Well, I'm sorry I didn't mean to insult you Ashley it's just that … " Then she interupted him and said "Oh I know, I know … It's your wife isn't it?" And she got back up and got close to him again, then said "Well maybe you wouldn't mind if I pretended to be her for you." You knew I was in love when I first saw you? I just couldn't take my eyes off of you and I wanted to get close to you right then and there ya know?" As she's twirling her hair with her leg on his leg. He said "Ashley!" She said, "With all due respect Mr. Dean, I want to be with you tonight, can I?" He said … "Ashley!" and she said "Yes I like when you say my name like that". So he then said "Ashley. … I have to go now." And He ran out of the room. She yelled "But wait, what about your lasagna!" As she followed him down the stairs. She said "Okay, wait a minute Mr. Dean I'm really sorry for that, I don't know what's gotten into me lately but …"

He said "There is really no need for that Ashley I think I really must go now. You told me to give you a chance on this date and I did." I like to keep my morals in tact." And she said "No, it's just because of your wife isn't it?!" As she was looking for a way to bring an accusation against him. He said "You keep speaking about my wife and I keep away from you permanently." And she said "Okay I'm sorry, with all due respect Mr. Dean, I'm not the one who sinned and then self-proclaimed myself as a Christian." He came close to her and addressed her sternly without leaving any inch of space between them he said; "What sin did I do exactly

Ashley? Huh? Tell me exactly what it is so I can repent because if I did, then it sure wasn't worth the time." And he quickly left the house and slammed the door on her face. And once he got out he thought "Oh man, I forgot to get the picture, so he went back, and knocking on the door he said "Wait a minute, can I please have just one small taste of that lasagna?" And she slammed the door back in his face and locked it. As he snapped his fingers and left, Ashley went back into the room trying to see how she would get him to sign those papers seeing that this plan didn't work. And now knowing that he knew Rebecca, she sure didn't want to miss that chance to see Becc again, so she called him and left voicemail knowing that he probably wouldn't answer saying …

"Hey Mr. Dean, I'm really sorry about everything that happened, and yea, I know I said sorry a few times before but I really wanna give it another shot with you. There's something special about you that I haven't been around or seen in a really long time in a person and I just want to assure you that it wouldn't ever get out of hand like that again. But, I'm really sorry." So Ashley was being genuine in her apology to Mr. Dean, but her motives were still in the wrong place. She still didn't want to submit to do what was right and so she pressed on the more in her attempt to get his business handed over to her. Thinking that it would gratify her and make her feel content. So later on, Mr. Dean got the message and was very happy to hear her apology but still had some concerns within himself about her. So he decided to take action to figure out if that picture on the wall was indeed Rebecca. He kept feeling bothered in his mind about that picture. He saw Rebecca and he said to her "Hey Becc, how's it going?" She said "Hey Dad it's fine, how's it going with you?" He said to her … "Well, I thought about something. I really wanted my date to meet Natalie and it just bothered me how that whole thing went down." She said "Oh don't worry about that Dad I'm sure she totally understands, you don't have to bother yourself about that, she'll meet her oneday hopefully. Do you think that she's the right one? Oh how did the date go by the way?" And he said, well to be honest, no not exactly, I don't think she's the right one at all … In fact, she's totally wrong. But to give a little credit, she does have a way with words." So they both laughed and He said "Becca, I don't mean to intrude into your past personal life but I just wanna ask.. Do you remember taking a picture with your friend from a while back? The one that caused you all that trouble?" And she said "Yea, I'm sure we took pictures together more than one, why do you ask Dad?" (*She calls him Dad*) And he said "Well, what about this do you remember being in the woods having on a green top blue jeans and bangs with your friends arm wrapped around your neck.. Both of you having the peace sign up?"

She says "Yea, actually I was very small then.. Have you seen that picture?" If so where is it so I can burn it!" He laughed out loud and said "Well wait a minute you don't have to worry about doing that I just wanted to know that's all." She said "hmm. Okay …" So he said "No need to worry, If I see it again, now I'll know what to do with it!" So she said "Okay thanks Dad." And walked away. Now he was considering meeting back up with Ashley again to find out the truth about the whole situation. He wanted to see if she was playing games with him and to trap her in her own game. So the next two days he decided to call her back and he apologized for his actions, and slamming the door on her face. Now he was being sincere in his apology, but he wanted to see what type of game she was up to by inviting him over and trying to go on a date in knowing that it was Ashley's old friend. He was really convinced that this Ashley and Rebecca's friend, was indeed the same Ashley. So he started the investigation by agreeing to her voicemail proposal in having the second date. He didn't really wanna get Rebecca and Natalie involved in it, even though he thought about it. He decided that he wanted to do this all by himself. So they set out for the date. They made it for 2 days from then, and this time it would be at her house from the beginning till the end. He was determined to get to that picture and nobody's lousy lasagna was going to stop him.

Two days went by when he picked up the phone to call Ashley and see if she was ready for him to come over. (*As you can imagine, she had some tricks up her sleeve for date number two to go exactly how she planned it.*) So he came over to her house dressed in a casual outfit, with another blazer on. And Ashley had on a dazzling sparkled gold dress and a face packed with blush makeup; sparkled earrings and big loose wig of curls and she had tucked her bangs in at this point. She looked like she was going to perform at a show. So when he came to the door, she opened it and said "Well hello, how do you do my friend?" With a big smile on her face and he was tickled as he walked inside, squinting his eyes because of all of the bright festive lights she had on in the house this time. She even hung up her chandelier and had all different kinds of holiday ornaments with it as if it were christmas. She had up bright, clear christmas bulbs in and all of the lights were on, and the fire place was lit. I mean the place was so bright that he could hardly see to walk inside. So he saw the picture of Ashley and Rebecca clearly when he walked in. The dining room table was full of food for a family size. She had a huge fried turkey. Mashed potatoes, collard greens, squash, hot wings, Fresh oven baked bread, Macaroni and cheese, ham, yams, stuffing and she even had out a specialty salad bar, I mean you would have thought that it were thanksgiving. But she took off his blazer for him and began to hang it up when she said, "hold on a minute and take off your shoes." By then he had enough and said "Ashley, this isn't what I had to do last time; what happened?" And she laughed and said "Silly, that's because I wanna make a new start with you." So he said "You really did go out of your way for me didn't you?" As he began to doubt that she had any wrong intentions.

She said, "Yes, and I did it just for you this time." He started to feel bad about his plan to trick her into confessing the truth about herself and Rebecca and he started to think that maybe she did really like him. So at that very moment, he decided to give her another shot and a fresh start. Once he sat in his chair, the music started playing instantly and this big gust of theatre smoke came from out of the living room, so he was startled and looked around over his shoulder and said "This is too much". But she didn't pay him any mind. She Brought out a bottle of champagne, 2 glasses, and then sat across from him in her chair. So she poured the champagne in his glass first and then in hers. He said "Ashley, you sure are entertaining I can admit that." And a name to remember … And she said, "Well, I think I like to call it "Fun". And he clicked the remote to another station (being that it was on his side of the table) he turned to a Gospel station; put down the remote, and said to her "You like this station right? I mean, is it okay with you?" She said "Yea sure that's fine for me I like it!" So she asked if he wanted her to make his plate and he insisted that he was fine and he would make it. They sat there and talked for about an hour and a half. Then they were done laughing, talking and eating and he complemented her on the food and thanked her for the extra work she went out of her way to do for him. Ashley got up and started dancing to the music and she knew the song that came on so she started singing along to it. Mr. Dean was only looking at Ashley to make sure she was sober. So she laughed and said "I know this song and I know alot of other gospel songs but, wouldn't you rather hear something else?" so she went to grab the remote and said … "Hear, let me see that remote for a second." As she switched the channel to a reggae station then started dancing again but this time, she was jumping and clapping loud too. He was amused by her being so entertaining and saw everything that she was doing as efforts to impress him.

So he stood up to go throw his plate away when all of a sudden she yelled at him "Hey, get back over here Mr." And then he really started to question if she was actually drunk. (*But she wasn't drunk; she was only pretending to be under influence to see how he would react.*) So he came over to her and said. Ashley why don't you have a seat for a little while and clear your head. And she said "You clear your plate, now you want me to clear my head ahhahha." So then he moved her to the chair and sat her down. He explained to her. "I've only been here for a little while now and you have gotten drunk already, So I guess you were drinking before I came in. What could be the matter? You can talk to me." And she said "Nothing's the matter I just wanna have fun." So they just sat across from eachother distant. By then he already turned the music down, and was planning on leaving soon. He got out of his chair and came over to her to say, Ashley, I wanna ask you a question and I want you to be completely honest with me; can you do that? She said "Well Mr. Dean, all this time you should know by now I am an honest girl" and she smiled. And she continued … "I just wanna say something, you are the cutest thing that I've ever seen." So he asked her. … "Ashley do you know that picture I saw in the hallway when you first walk in with who I believe is you and a young girl with your arm wrapped around her neck?" She said "Oh no Mr. Dean here we go again" He said "Yea, here we go. Would you mind telling me the truth about who she is?" He didn't want to waste any more time trying to figure out who this girl was. So she answered him "I told you who she was, it's my friend Stacey."

She continued … "You must think she's really hot don't you because you sure do keep asking about her." He said, it's really not a matter of "hot" Ashley it's just that …" She cut him off and said shh shh, you don't have to explain anything to me, I know already you just want more than one." She went on … "I know Mr. Dean, I've met men like you before and all they want is more than one girl because they feel unsettled in their relationship and me and you have just gotten started so I'm gonna call Stacey right now and invite her over." As she picked up her phone and pretended to call he yelled "No, no, no, that wouldn't be neccessary it's alright Ashley, nevermind." So she insisted, "No, you keep asking me about my picture and I want to assure you that she is well of age now and ready to …" And he cut her off and said "That's enough It's really alright, you don't have to call her." Then he said "Come on and dance like you were doing, it's fine …" He started thinking to himself that maybe it was a coincidence or that they had a similar pictures. So he decided to leave the picture issue alone for now since she was attempting to call her friend. He pulled her back up out of her chair and began to swing dance with her and talk. And as they were swinging, he thought of something, He grabbed the picture off of the wall and swung her downwards. While her head was still yet facing backwards towards the floor, he snuck the picture in his pocket and then kept dancing with her. He swung her back up and started dancing more towards the kitchen. Then he tempted her to begin to look for an argument so that the truth would come out.

So they went in the kitchen and he said "Let's play police. You be the bad guy and I'll place you in handcuffs. So she said "Well, well now I see you coming out of your shell finally." He said, "Yea, and it's about that time I did." So she took it as a green light for her and him to be together but he said, "Oh wait, on second thought … My wife." So she got irritated and said "Your wife?" don't you think about anything else besides her? Besides, she's not here it's just me and you." He said to her "How could you say that? You don't even know what kind of woman she was." (As he let her go from holding onto her." And she yelled "Ok I'm sick of this, this is pathetic and weak. Your wife has nothing on me." So he got angry with her and said "Really? Is that how you feel? What if it was someone you cared about, then it wouldn't be so easy to talk bad about them huh Ashley?" She said "Well it's not" and she cursed his wife saying that she was getting in the way of her and him.

So as bad as he wanted to slap her in the face, he decided that now was the perfect time to see just who it was that was in that picture. He turned on the stove, and while it was lit, He placed a corner of the picture on the heat and told her to "look at it" and tell him who it was. So she says "Oh WOW it is Stacey! what is wrong with you?! She says "Okay, okay I take back everything I said. "And he said tell me who it is now!" At this point she was jumping over him, trying to catch the picture while his other arm was blocking her down. He kept saying "tell me, tell me", while she started to cry and when he saw her love for the picture, he thought about Rebecca and how she would be at a disadvantage again being in the company of Ashley if this was indeed the Ashley that Rebecca cried over losing. So he tricked her and said "Rebecca is not the one to be missed, You are! as he began to rip the picture, she cried "Rebecca!!! Nooooooo!!!" and he stopped and blew the picture off and said oh ok now I see your love for her. What is it that you want Ashley Tell me now." And she had mascara smeared all on her face looking down to the ground and she looked back up then said, all I really want is just the picture Mr. Dean. Stacey is my only friend I have.

So he said Stacey? but you just admitted it was Rebecca. so she lied even more and said, I only said that name because you said it, but the girls name is Stacey." (As she sniffled and wiped her tears away.) *By this time, he was really heated for not getting a satisfying answer.* … So Mr. Dean decided to keep the picture for himself until he reached Rebecca again, and their party had ended, so it was time for him to go home. He felt unsuccessful at his investigation and angry that his wife was insulted too. Ashley wouldn't budge. He had mixed feelings about Ashley and how to deal with her in regards to finding out if she was telling the truth. He left and went home. He flew out of his car and into his house screaming Rebecca! Rebecca where are you? This crazy big house!" "Rebecca where are you?" Crazy stairs … "As he flew straght to the back room and down into one of the basements of the house he yelled Rebecccaaaaaaaa!" And Kevin was down there and said "Dad why are you screaming Rebecca like that? She's not here. "So he said "I need to know where Rebecca is right now!" As he raced back up the stairs Kevin called him and said "Have you even tried calling her to see where she was?" So he paused from racing and started walking slow and was embarrassed. He said "I would've thought of that if you'd given me time Kevin. And Kevin laughed a little bit and said okay please take it easy Dad. By then he made it up the stairs and then proceeded to called her.

So meanwhile, Rebeccas's phone rings and she picks up … "Hello, Dad?" he said "Becc! where are you?" And she said "leaving the train station with some friends headed back to your house." So he said "Great, perfect! I got something I wanna show you so please come straight here." She said "Okay". Now as time went on, Ashley knew that he would ask Rebecca about the picture and find out, so she decided that she was gonna take it upon herself to go meet him at his house to try and stop him. Seeing that her initial mission wasn't accomplished yet, she quickly rushed out of her door to check his house and see if he was home; And he was home. But to come inside the entrance, she needed a gate key since it was late. So she decided to wait until somebody was coming either in or out to go inside after them. And about 15 mins after waiting, Rebecca pulls right in, inside of a taxi, so she gasps and says "Rebecca to herself and waits for her to get in, then pulls in behind her, making sure the gate will stay open position so that she could leave time for Rebecca to get inside the house. And then once Rebecca walked in, she drove on through making way for the taxi to leave. The mansion had a very long driveway on 2 sides with a set of gates; one on each side of it. To the right side of the mansion was where Ashley and Rebecca came in, the other side was left empty. It was about a 7 minute jog to get from the end of either of the gates to the door of the mansion. So Ashley parked the car down the hill and behind the trees as she hid behind a bush, inching her way up to the door behind Rebecca. Rebecca had already walked inside the door when Ashley came running behind her to ring the bell.

So once she was up to the door and rang the bell, Kevin came to the door and opened it. He didn't quite recognize her at the time and he just said "Yes, how may I help you?" So Ashley said, "I just came here to talk to your Dad (assuming that he knew who she was). Then he said "My Dad?" She said "Yes, your dad." So he then asked her "Who are you?" She responded "Ashley" He said "Okay, just wait here a moment." So he went to go get his dad as he started to remember her face, (being as though they were at the door except this time he was standing on the inside and she was on the out.) He recognized her at the moment he was about to call his dad when he said "That is the same Ashley that was Rebecca's friend." So He marched back towards the main door, and asked her "What are you doing here Ashley?" and she said "Nothing, nothing much just out hanging around on this side of town passing through. how about you?" So he didn't think her humor was funny and said "What do you want with my Dad

Ashley? We have no business with you." She turned her head to the side and underneath her breath mumbled "not yet.." But he overheard her and said "Not yet? You mean not ever!" And he slammed the door and went to see his Dad. He said "Dad? Dad, where are you? This crazy woman is at the door and she's looking for you!" So he said "I'm in here son. What crazy woman would this be?" So he said "Ashley". And he jumped up from the table and ran to the door." Kevin followed shortly after him and his Dad to open the door and said "What do you want Ashley and why are you here?" So she insisted that she was only there to talk things over with him. (Seeing that Kevin had already seen her, she tried to figure her way out of the situation.) Kevin and his Dad spoke with eachother and he said "Do you know her?" Kevin said Yes, this is Rebecca's old friend we told you about." So he said "Oh so it's true?"

Ashley couldn't deny at that point, but she knew that she would somehow see Rebecca close up if she hung around long enough and if they didn't close the door. So she finally admitted to it and begged them not to tell Rebecca about anything that happened. Mr. Dean asked her "So what was the point of all of this? to see Rebecca or to get her back in some kind of way?" She insisted that she was sincere about seeing him and wanting to get to know him. She even told them the truth finally about how she didn't know Rebecca was now a part of their family and about how she didn't know Mr. Dean was Kevin's Dad. But he didn't believe her or anything she said at this point. He told her that if she was serious about any of her life, she would leave immediately. And they saw her car parked behind the bushes and said "And what's up with you and your car being behind the bushes?" So she didn't respond, she just kept her head down and looked back. She turned around slowly and started to walk off with her head down as if she were sad. So they both slightly closed the door together; until there was a small crack in the door and they both looked at eachother. They didn't know what to think of the situation. They just kept starring at eachother until Kevin said out loud "I mean, she is still human.." His Dad replied "What could she have wanted all this time playing games like this." and then he thought to himself again; "Well, what if she was telling the truth this time?"

So he called her to come back to see if she would try and change her story again. She came back and walked slowly, then when her head was bent down, she looked up, (Kevin had walked away at that point). He said to her "What do you like about me that you would go through all of this trouble just to spend time with me?" So Ashley said "It's not that I don't like you anymore Mr. Dean, it's just takes a while to get to know me and many times, people already think that they have me figured out." He stopped her there and said "Well, we just argued and you weren't hesitant about trying to be confrontational with me." She said "Well, you weren't hesitant about it either Mr. Dean." And he didn't know what to say. Ashley had his words caught up in a knot. But she knew that she wasn't getting out of it that easy and that she must keep progressing through the conversation. So she started to adlib. She asked Mr. Dean "Do you remember when you said you all of these nice and sympathetic sweet things to me? I meant the words I spoke Mr. Dean. And even though the situation is the way it is, I know that God makes a beautiful thing out of things that are messed up."

She said.. "What would it take to finally get you to know that I am here, I have these problems but that I still know how to love and I still want to be around people. I have a big house and yet I'm all alone. (*As she places her hand over top of her head as if she were to faint.*) So he said to her "Ashley, if this is a game, I really don't want any more part in it."

"What were you thinking coming to my door in this way? Do you know I have security? "In the meantime, Kevin went to go find Rebecca. And He found her, then said "Ashley's outside ... And the same way we had her put in cuffs is the same way she's begging for us to take her back in cuffs. So the three ran upstairs to see her, but at this point, she had went back behind the tree and into her car. Mr. Dean was inside and turned around with the door closed behind his back when everyone was up stairs looking for Ashley. Kevin came running down the long hallway to the door first. He said "Where's Ashley, where did she go?" But Mr. Dean was bothered by the situation this time, so he said "Don't worry about it anymore, the girl is gone." He went on.. "She told me that she used to be a good girl and how everybody used to treat her badly but she was always the considerate, caring one. So they were all near him at this point and looked at eachother, then looked at him. So Kevin yelled out "Dad, really?!" He continued on and said "Don't start getting feelings for this girl now!" As Kevin swings the front door open and looks for Ashley. His dad said, "She's gone Kevin, and this time for good."

Ashley had driven to a different spot but she stood at the mansion, waiting to see if Rebecca would come out.

She waited and waited until she heard Rebecca coming outside with Natalie talking about finding out a way to meet up with Ashley to get to the bottom of this and to see how she was doing. Becc, said "I don't know what Mr. Dean said to her but the way he acted, seems like he she really hurt him." Natalie said "Yea, either that or he still likes her." So they both decided to try and investigate the situation to see what Ashley was trying to get out of this so it wouldn't persist any longer. And they wanted to make sure Mr. Dean's heart wouldn't be involved in her for long. So they made it their buisness to go over to her house first thing in the morning and try to talk her down. While Ashley was still outside of the house, they had finished talking and went back in. So she decided to leave at this point to go back home, and when she got there, she was so dissapointed in herself for ruining the plan and not being able to get him to sign the papers like she wanted that she didn't know what to do. She went to her room and started rolling around on her bed and fighting the bed and having weird jitters then her eyes began to roll to the back of her head and she yelled out curse words.

So after the episode stopped, she went to take a bath and when she got in, she lit a cigarette and sat there with an angry face flicking on and off music channels in her bathroom's studio. She didn't know what to do with herself the rest of that evening so she just sat there gazing until she ended up falling to sleep in the bathtub. The next morning, she heard her doorbell ring so she hopped out of the tub and put on her robe. She ran downstairs to the door and saw that it was Rebecca and Natalie. She was shocked. They kept ringing and knocking as she didn't answer they yelled, "Ashley, we want to talk to you!" She was so suprised and didn't know what to say but she wouldn't open the door in fear. So she just sat behind the door and yelled "Go away." So they started talking to her at the door and pleading with her. Rebecca said "Look Ashley, we know what happened, and we know how you might feel right now so we just want to talk." And Ashley responded and told her "Well it's funny you want to talk to me now. Out of all people, you". "Ashley open up the door." Rebecca said, but she wouldn't. So Natalie told her that they wouldn't be leaving until she opened up. And they sat there on her porch.

So After a while, they saw that she wouldn't budge and decided to call Mr. Dean. By then, Ashley had her music blasting inside of the house as she was getting dressed and continuing on with her day. Rebecca called Mr. Dean anyway. "Hello" She said. "Hey Becc, what's going on? How are you my dear?" She said "Hey Dad, were at Ashley's house." He said "What!? What are you doing there? What's going on?" So Becca continued, "Well, me and Natalie decided that we would come here and get to the bottom of things to straighten this whole thing out. She was our problem in the first place, not yours." So he said "I want you two to leave now, you shouldn't be back over there stirring up anymore confusion. Everything is already a mess. Let's just leave Ashley alone and everything will be fine." So Natalie grabbed the phone and she said "Dad, we want you to come here; Please." "We really think this is a good idea, that way she won't come up with any more plans and she can leave our family alone." He said "Alright, look my break is at noon. If you guys are still there by then I can swing by there. I don't know what will come of this but I'm hoping that you have a good plan." And he hung up.

So the two just sat there. At that time it was 10:00. They waited there for 2 hours and then decided to call Mr. Dean back to see if he was ready to take his lunch break. So he answered and said "Yes girls, I'm coming." And he headed to the house. During the time the girls were still there, Ashley kept peeping out of the peephole, and was considering leaving through the basement door or out of the backdoor. But she didn't come out, she just stood there at the peep hole when all of a sudden, she sees Mr. Dean pulling up in her driveway. He got out and said "Alright you two, what is it? What's the plan?" So they said "Let's go inside and maybe you'll be able to get her to open the door. So they tried ringing the door again, and this time she told them that if they didn't leave she would call the police. So Mr. Dean was angry at that point and said. "Hey Ashley ... Didn't you come hassling me when I went to go jog around my homee? Do you remember that? And did you not come ringing my door bell to ask me for another chance?

I really started to care about you, even yesterday after you left, I was worried about you. Now you have my 2 Angels here outside worried about you but you insist that we just go away? Don't you understand that you have a problem that needs to be taken care of?

Just tell me what it was that you were seeking all this time and we'll leave you alone."

So Ashley just sat there thinking of what she could say next. Meanwhile, thinking about how she missed Rebecca. She responded ... "Rebecca can come in ... & then I'll talk" So they looked at eachother and said Oh so it was about Rebecca ... They all decided that Rebecca should go in even after the last incident, they had come up with a plan just incase Ashley tried something stupid. So she proposed that Rebecca come through one of the side doors to get in, and she did. She came in and Ashley was there with her head down and a bashful look on her face. She said "I miss you". Rebecca said "Ashley, you have got to stop." She walked up close to Ashley and said "You have got to change your ways and get to know who God is. If you don't stop and submit your ways to God, then you are in for something that could have been avoided. Jesus died to give you life and is still reaching out to you. Even now. Don't you know?? Don't refuse Him." And she ended it there and as she was about to turn and walk out, Ashley grabbed her by the shoulder and turned her back to say "I love you Rebecca". So Rebecca said "Love is in action, not in words." She continued ... "If you love me, you would love all of me.. even my true self and who God has shown me that I really am in Him."

So she responded sarcastically "Well ... who are you?" and Rebecca said "God knows who I am, my identity is found in Him." But you, do you know who you are? Can you sleep at night?" And Ashley remembered how she wasn't able to sleep because of the jitters and weird things that were happening to her. She also remembered a few dreams, so she insisted that she please stay with her. But Rebecca wanted to tell her one last time how God showed her that it really wasn't her, but all of the things that she experienced were for her learning too. She was shown her lifestory and given understanding to many things. Rebecca told her how He can show her, her's too if she would just give her life to Christ. Finally, Rebecca parted ways with Ashley and the whole family ended up leaving Ashley's house. Ashley still wouldn't change her ways and she just kept getting worse and worse. But in the end the family got to see how much they needed eachother. Ashley is like many people today who don't understand the power that they use is for their hurt. Mind manipulation and playing games with peoples lives only fill the doers up with a void. It is an example of how we all need eachother on this walk of life and how God puts things in place for us to take a hold of; and it all works out for each of our well being. Fin

THE STIMULANT

These were the words that I heard oneday while I was having alone time with The Lord. After getting rudly interrupted with some feelings that weren't pleasant, plus other mind hassles and things like that which come with getting that connection flowing. These are the natural feelings that occur, so I'm not going to pretend; but just because we have these feelings, do they mean we should embrace them in the wrong way? Once these feelings hit, do you know what to do with them? God expects us to give them to Him. Though He is the supplier of all things good, those arousing feelings, given to share between a married man and woman, are made for that married man and woman. He truly made ALL things to be good. It is absolutely amazing how God connects so well with each one of us on such a personal level. He even connects to us in ways we would never imagine too; just that sometimes we hang onto the things or feelings that we like so much, it makes it hard for Him to move us off of it. Just like that of a feeling we get when we express a form of marital love. Think of a child playing a sport with thier father. They are so into this sport and even learned a few new things but all the while his Dad is trying to take him to have ice cream and then to go play a different sport. This kid doesn't know that his Dad is about to take him to go tour the world next week so when his Dad says it's time to rap up the game, he consistently throws a temper tantrum not knowing that he may be ruining the trip his Father planned. He shows us to rather trust than fuss.

So back to it at hand. These are the Words That He spoke to me after getting those feelings While seeking Him.

"I am the stimulant the root of Jesse the tribe of Benjamin If any man hunger come after me, if any man thirst my well is full." God wanted me to write this down and before I had knowledge of the scripture meaning, He told me this, so I went to go check out what the scripture is saying. It's in Isaiah 11:10 "And in that day there shall be a root of Jesse, which shall stand for an ensign of the people, to it shall the Gentiles seek: and His rest shall be glorious." Smh..Wow, that is a powerful scripture right there..God tells us that, the stimulant we all search for or even the thrill we might seek in life, whether it be from a person, place or thing, He is the one that provides it. We sometimes seek after it in different ways. A stimulant that comes between a man and a woman in marriage, Yep, God provides that. It was meant for beauty not for ashes. Since the thought of it has been made to seem so corrupted over time (due to the media exploiting it like it's a fashion,) The beauty in what God created has vanished and people are still looking for that and feel like they have to do it often or to different people to get that "Rush". Well that isn't true.

The stimulant that God provides is pure and undefiled. It is thrilling and exciting and leaves you joyous, yet it is Holy. If people lack self control in general, and enduldge themselves or misuse the beautiful things in which God has given us, then they will lack self-control when God gives us understanding of His love He freely shares with all of us, as Our Father; but God is trying to teach us. God warns us that if you do not live a repentant life-style in Him, how you will perish. Nothing is made to be corruptive but satan is the one that corrupted it. Many of us (because of the deceiver) are searching for it in the wrong ways. He revealed to me that He is that stimulant we are searching for. Our life is the thrill that we seek when we want to go out, even if it's just to the mall. We start to see it plain when we live it in Him.

We see how His love lasts and the devil uses things to try and take your heart from what God shows you. It is a journey to fight for it back. But now, we have to pick up the pace because of "stage fright". When you hear stage fright, normally you relate it to being on stage, afraid of the crowd but this can also be related to spiritual growth. We have to reach certain stages in our growth with The Lord so we will be like Him when He returns. And, we may be experiencing high levels of contraction during spiritual birthing periods. So it can seem frightening, but God knows all. He wants us to hold onto His hand as we go through these levels and not to look at the world, or even look like the world.

SELF-MADE INTELLECT VS. DO YOU KNOW THAT JESUS CHRIST IS IN YOU?

We are full of intellect by nature, it's just a matter of what we choose to put in our minds. Sometimes though, people change thier natural intellect and put them on self-made intellectual standards, when they don't keep fully pursuing God; therefore placing a limit on themselves by not pushing through to do the right thing given us by nature. Let's say a child has an ant farm. Ants like to move and the child has a choice to block the ants in a cage or to let them go on a ramp. The child decides to block them in a cage. That child has just limited his intellect by feeding into the corrupt nature of sin because he chose to use the strategy of power instead of relying on love. That child made non-verbal communication to the ants inflicting power over the ants, forgetting that God has power over him. Now that was just a child but, when we are hurt or even when we just want to express our power given by God, we have a tendency to gravitate towards control when we feel uncertain about something or when we simply get annoyed, and various other reasons. God is in us, So how come we don't go after Him in the ways of the men of old? Because honestly, our hearts are sometimes in too many of the wrong places unfortunately. We are weighed down with society's spiritual junk food & cover our natural art we get from God, and simply settle for less. By nature, we think higher than society limits us, but most times we go lower to please man. Some people plunge themselves in alcoholic beverages or turn to some other source of junk. Why not seperate from the things of this world and turn to please God? well yes, it is hard but our best and most desirable fruits come from when we don't adlib, (or think too much), Remember Martha? If you don't know, the story of Martha can be found in Luke 10 especially verse 42, where Martha was so busy cleaning up, doing dishes, fixing herself, the house, probably the furniture maybe clothes needed to be washed, etc. etc.. While Mary just sat underneath Jesus all day not lifting up a finger; So Jesus tells Martha that Mary was doing good by staying up underneath His feet.

(SCRIPTURE Luke 10:38-42 KJV) "As Jesus and his disciples were on their way, he came to a village where a woman named Martha opened her home to him. 39 She had a sister called Mary, who sat at the Lord's feet listening to what he said. 40 But Martha was distracted by all the preparations that had to be made. She came to him and asked, "Lord, don't you care that my sister has left me to do the work by myself? Tell her to help me!" 41 "Martha, Martha," the Lord answered, "you are worried and upset about many things, 42 but few things are needed—or indeed only one.[f] Mary has chosen what is better, and it will not be taken away from her."

We do good when we do that! Some might argue well how will anything get done? Well, the principal thing, is to stay underneath Jesus and the rest comes to pass because He is the only way we know anything through the Holy Spirit.

(SCRIPTURE 1 Co.2:11 KJV) says. "For what man knoweth the things of a man, save the spirit of man which is in him?." Now when we go all out of our way trying to please man, we loose the originality of the thing and then it becomes luke-warm. You put on lotion when your legs are dry but who told you that you need a bottle of lotion? God wouldn't want us to go trusting in the bottle of lotion once we see that it's good for use, rather trust in God who told us that the bottle of lotion was good for use. Many times, we trust in the person, place or thing that God revealed to us that was good, and so we want IT, not considering how it wasn't that thing in the first place that we wanted, we all ultimately want JESUS! Now that we know Jesus is indeed the supplier of ALL things, wouldn't you wanna pamper Him? It is written in Psalm 2:12 "Kiss the Son, lest He be angry, and ye perish from the way." So we want to be up under Jesus as much as possible seeing that He is the Giver of All. Once we are born again, we have the mind of Christ so, anything we try to do on our own without the Spirit of God's help becomes fleshly, even in doing His own works.

(SCRIPTURE 1 Corinthians 2:16 KJV) "For who hath known the mind of the Lord that he may instruct him? But we have the mind of Christ." "Or do you not know that your body is the temple of The Holy Spirit in you, whom you have from God? And you are not your own." SCRIPTURE 1 Co. 6:19 KJV. So intellect is not bad, it's just more to it than that. The intellect that comes from The Holy Spirit is no doubt the best, just like He says, He is the supplier of All needs and we wouldn't want any other! Do we really believe that God made ALL? Well, how come we go against the things that God said He would take vengence in? He told us that His Angels will seperate the wheat from the tares. We do these things because of fear. We all have a calling and a purpose in our lives for God and when these things strike us, we have to turn to Jesus to always know how to handle them. Our duty is not to take vengance, but to preach the Word of God in understanding. In season and out of season, yes and we also reprove, rebuke and exhort! Sometimes we reprove or rebuke without good understanding. We reprove or rebuke the work of

God we get scriptures but still don't understand what we really mean or if it's even one hundred percent accurate because we may not have the right motives. When we do things based on the right motives, (and we know the only "right" motives come from God our Savior), but it's the same way. We do things naturally by the Spirit without understanding! But God shows us later on what exactly that thing means. There is an example in Scripture for what I'm revealing through The Holy Spirit but this scripture is relating to those who don't know God, who act, move and have their being because of God, just like we all do and they don't give God the Glory because they don't know Him. Romans 2:14 "For when the Gentiles, which have not the law, do by nature the things contained in the law, these having not the law, are a law unto themselves". So we know that some people by nature show the characteristics of God, but to do the works of God are beyond us; and that is why He gave us His HOLY SON! Only being a part of God are we able to do His works, so His Son left us His Holy Spirit! When we really believe that Jesus saved us, we know that we now have His eyes, So we are not bound to the old testament laws even as Jesus came and showed us. We keep them according to our individual lives to know that they are good. But we don't law bind ourselves or others to the things that are within the old testament. We do according to what Our Lord tells us through The Holy Spirit. It is written down and understood that Jesus went into the corn fields on the Sabbath Day and His disciples plucked the ears of the corn when the pharisees saw that, they were mad and thought they were breaking the law of Moses which tells us not to do a work on the Sabbath, (preparing food or being out in the fields getting food is indeed considered a work on the sabbath), But what did Jesus say? He said to leave them alone and told them that He is The Lord of the Sabbath and we know that when we go to Him and live and abide in Him that we are indeed keeping the

Sabbath and He also lets us know that it is good to do well on the Sabbath. We keep The laws of the old testament When we truly love Jesus with all of our heart mind and soul and love others as ourselves. And if we love Jesus truly, we spend time with Him and keep His commandments, We do what is natural, but spending so much time with Him, we start to really know and understand that He doesn't beat us up over the heads for our mistakes. So you see it's all about a relationship with our Father through The Lord! He knows, so we know that we are human and make mistakes and that Jesus saved us from them! We judge according to mercy and not unto condemnation. And every single thing goes back to Jesus! We love John 3:16 and we also love John 3:17 KJV which tells us, "For God sent not His Son into the world to condemn the world; but that the world through Him might be saved."

(SCRIPTURE Ephesians 2:15 KJV) "Having abolished in His flesh the enmity, even the law of commandments contained in ordinances ; for to make in Him self of twain one new man, so making peace"

Jesus came to make all things clean according to His purpose; and when Peter refused to eat that "unclean" bird which was flying in the air, God told him specifically not to call something that unclean, that He made clean.

(SCRIPTURE) "And the voice spake unto him again the second time, What God hath cleansed, that call not thou common." Acts 10:15 The old testament being fufilled by Jesus, He proved in showing mercy that some things are acceptable according to the law. He shows us in (SCRIPTURE Mark 2:23 KJV), that HE IS the fufilment of the law by proving to the pharisees of what is acceptable to God, who Himself made the sabbath day despite the ordinances and religous practices put into place by (God/Himself) through Moses. He came to show us what is acceptable and good in an unholy world. God made it possible for us to go, according to our own individual lives through The Holy Spirit, Now only God can do that! Jesus is our Mercy! And in (SCRIPTURE Mark 7:18 KJV) God again shows us how meats do not enter into our heart but only into our stomach, it is just food, and all meats are declared clean to us now.

Religous people and non-belivers alike, follow down behind the old testament laws by keeping the commandments and doctrines of men. They say that you can't eat certain meats, or create laws like not being able to eat without unwashed hands etc., things that all men can't accept everywhere; basically putting laws on mankind that are too self-righteous, and neglecting mercy because of self-satisfaction; which also leaves out the fact that God did everything for us! He showed us what is acceptable in His sight and proved by mercy that certain laws couldn't be upheld for all-men everywhere so He gave us His Precious and Mighty SON! God told them that if they don't accept His Son, they will die in their sins; and we can't keep the law by ourselves because it leaves us solely bound to the law and neglects people in other places and various kinds of situations! Thank God for Jesus!

(SCRIPTURE KJV Titus 1:15 KJV) "Unto the pure, all things are pure: but unto them that are defiled and unbelieving is nothing pure; but even their mind and conscience is defiled."

(SCRIPTURE 1 Co 10:23 KJV) "All things are lawful for me, but all things are not expedient: all things are lawful for me, but all things edify not."

Now this Scripture was referencing meats but we know that when he mentions "all things", we don't limit God, knowing that He is the author and finisher of All things indeed. For He says

(SCRIPTURE Isaiah 45:7 KJV) "I form the light, and create darkness: I make peace, and create evil: I the LORD do all these things." And in (SCRIPTURE 1 Co 10:23 KJV) He was also testifying how all things are indeed God's, but some things are not useful for edifying the Kingdom even though all things are lawful for me to use. God shows us what things are useful for us vs. what is not useful. After John, (being in the wilderness) came; Then our Savior Jesus (who came humbly) came, to show us that we are not Holy anymore by being like the prophets of old in the form of outward appearance; ex: covering our faces, sacrifices by the flesh and things like that, because He came as our ultimate sacrifice, so now in our flesh, nothing can save us. The flesh is the old corrupt form of man, but once we are living in the new man and our hearts are surrendered in Jesus, we now have a veil we have put on, in our hearts. That goes back to where He says not to call things unclean that He has made clean. Our veil is Jesus! His seal reveals the things that are clean and permissible by Him.

(SCRIPTURE 2 Corinthians 3:13 KJV) "And not as Moses, which put a vail over his face, that the children of Israel could not stedfastly look to th end of that which is abolished:".

Tho we have outstanding capabilities in which we can see, and though we have come a long way, we still cannot reach the heart of God in our own form and fashion. We were given these things, these capabilities these qualities and each one of us play our part in making them stand out! But God knows that we only go up to a certain point with Him. Just like in the days of the Tower of Babel, we are building ourselves up to reach God, but God warns us that though were building, we will fall if we don't submit to Him and do it His way. He warns us that He is a jealous God and He is jealous for our love and attention.

(SCRIPTURE Hosea 13:6 KJV) "According to their pasture, they became satisfied, and being satisfied, their heart became proud; therefore they forgot me." Romans 1:21 "Because that when they knew God, they glorified Him not as God, neither were thankful; but became vain in their imaginations, and their foolish heart was darkened." (SCRIPTURE KJV Romans 10:3) "For they being ignorant of God's righteousness, and going about to establish their own righteousness, have not submitted themselves unto the righteousness of God." He makes miracles from out of the dust. So also does He make miracles out of man. We can never look at mankind above God who created him. We only use our capabilities God gives us for Him or against Him, because there are 2 works at play in this life. Those eternal works and those that will be burned up and have no matter. There is no in between. God warns us that His people perish for a lack of knowledge. Those are the things God is trying to teach us. But it is only His supernatural work that has to take place in our lives to help us see His ways and turn us from evil to good. We have to recognize our corrupt nature and know that we need a Holy God to cleanse and purify us. To think we are not uncorrupt is an error in itself; because we didn't make ourselves. We are not capable of purifying ourselves through our own flesh. If that were possible, we would be perfect. God shows us a true and lasting appreciation to His ways and order when we apply it to our lives, and those temporary things we want at a glance, tend to fall off of us and we see them for what they really are; not only that, but how we have been used and decieved by satan just like at the beginning. Jesus' whole point of guiding us was to tell us to come out of the flesh. Jesus is our road map for ALL things (SCRIPTURE.1 John 2:6 KJV) "He that says he abides in Him ought himself also to walk, even as He walked." And we must know that when God tells us to do it, He makes a provision, we just have to believe it.

OUR GIFTS

We can understand the rules and government of GOD when we really really really want to bad ... And when we do, we can get an understanding our very own history. Have you ever been to an amusement park as a kid and you wanted a toy, a funnel cake or cotton candy really really really bad? Our Father wants our attention in that way. When we truly abide in God, we know that we indefinitely have no rules and regulations, but everything is freely given to us; We realize the short term of our desires are limited to supply us temporarily through grace; And they only continuously leave us wanting more. Well, Our gifts go along with the rest of the promises of God, and they have their proper functions for proper times that God wants us to use them. He doesn't do anything small. If we want to use our gifts for a purpose other than God, it will only be on a small scale. Not to the level where God wants to bring us. None of us could ever come to our full potential when we limit ourselves for matters of this world. Especially when a Holy God has nothing to do with the carnal man. The flesh nature cannot please God. As said in (SCRIPTURE Romans 8:8 KJV) "So then they that are in the flesh cannot please God." It is written (SCRIPTURE 1 Co 15:50 KJV) "Flesh and blood cannot inherit the Kingdom."

It is written (SCRIPTURE 1 Co 15:53 KJV) "For this corruptible must put on incorruption and this mortal must put on imortality";

Because He paid the price for our fallen, corrupt, carnal state. So do we live in it's state to fufill it's desires? Not quite.

(SCRIPTURE Romans 8:5 KJV) "For they that are after the flesh do mind the things of the flesh; but they that are after the Spirit, the things of the Spirit".

When being in a Spiritual state, you are not high-minded resting in the fact that *God freely gives us ALL things.* Why should we fight to get to the top when He puts us there? A talent given by God, He wants to be used for His purposes, He is a Holy God. So while a person may not intentionally be trying to corrupt the rules, government and establishment of God, or use your gifts for evil, by default it is subjected to the carnal nature of man for the power and work of the enemy. Though it may look spotless, God says this (SCRIPTURE Hosea 4:6 KJV) "My people perish for a lack of knowledge; because thou hast rejected knowledge, I will also reject thee."

If they aren't chasing after Him, they won't know they are. God gives each one of us chances to come to know Him because He loves us more than we think or even know.

SEEDS OF FAITH

(INSERT SCRIPTURE) "Nevertheless I am continually with thee: thou hast holden me by my right hand" Psalms 73:23

Our love for The Lord grows as we continue to plant seeds of faith. Whatever seeds we sow in our life are the ones we will reap so by us sowing seeds to the Kingdom, we reap Heavenly Kingdom possesions.

(SCRIPTURE Gal 6:7 KJV) God tells us in His Word not to be decieved because whatever we sow we will reap. Well how can anybody do this? By faith and not by sight. He also tells us in (SCRIPTURE Gal 6:8 KJV) That whoever sows to his flesh will reap corruption but the one that sows to the spirit will reap eternal life. One of the fruits of the Spirit are faith, so that seed of faith can stretch with God when we exercise it. Excercising faith in God comes by asking Him for it.

(SCRIPTURE Matt 7:11 KJV) "How much more shall your Father which is in heaven give good things to them that ask Him" to grow in faith, exercise it through prayer. So when we genuinely apply the fruits of love, Joy, peace, longsuffering, gentleness, goodness, faith, meekness and temperance, as seen in (SCRIPTURE Gal 5:22 KJV), in our lives through Christ, we are sowing to the Spirit. As we go on our walk of faith, we realize that we start to get back for what we put out, and don't know understand or realize exactly how it happens. We have to trust that it's not in ourselves. God is the same today, yesterday and forever! When we grow Spiritually, it is because we chose to exercise the nature of The Son of God being lived out in us. Just like the nature of plants growing by way of the sun (which is the natural source of earth's energy to maintain it), Spiritually the same thing applies. And we by nature grow, from being in the presence of The Son, who is the ultimate source of All energy! "I am the vine, ye are the branches: He that abideth in me and I in him, the same bringeth forth much fruit: for without me ye can do nothing". The will of The Lord for the people of God is good. If we take time in our life's process but God is almost not able to reach the hearts of man due to the increase of intelligence, when simplicity is all we need. God takes care of the rest. Our time and our effort go to so many different things that it comes a time for neglect. We must neglect our family, our friends our social activites and everything we know and love and come to the meeting place with Christ. God just wants us to come to terms with who we really are in Him and to blossom for Him. We are really a chosen people called out for His purpose, we just have to believe it.

God made it possible to have children without having children. Even though things change in our society, The nature of God forever stays the same. So reproduction is in the form of life itself. We are only made after the image of God Himself so we know that we are also capable of making things reproduce. But, things have gotten way overboard throughout time. For example, cloning animals, robots and crazy stuff of that nature. But as much science and technology used today, we could never be God, nor should we desire to try to be. Tho we are made to be like the Image of His Son, we don't try and climb above Him, we follow behind Him! God stamps a key on our heart for good service in due time, and He will let us know we've done a well job and are His good and faithful servants because He loves us! God can produce/make us into something greater when we allow Him to through the power and work of The Holy Spirit. We have been made in a form that we don't understand the full meaning of nonetheless are unable to control becasue of death. Have you ever heard the doctor tell you or your friend that there is nothing they can do about it, or they don't know what it is yet, or they haven't found any problem? That is because as much technology as we have here in this world, doctors still cannot understand the full structure of human life. And when we aggressively take hold of/ handle these things we don't know much about but have free access to, they start to become a problem to us because of being handled in the wrong way. Eg; Adam and Eve. Nothing is limited to us, but God is God and He wants to show us how to use it! Even when we use these things, the nature of God can seem so estranged to us because of not fufilling His Divine purpose. ; A child starts off as a fetus, then grows into a human then grows into a full sized child ... To become a baby, to become a toddler to become a child to become a teen, to become an adult to become an elder. Now that's some serious science right there! That's a physical transformation right before our very eyes. And we will also continue to produce after this life, why do we settle when we all have that longing for something more? You see how much satan has decieved us so far? Through non-fictional stories, movies and so forth, the devil has made the things of God seem so estranged to us. He is even identifying what is right to be wrong. But God doesn't leave us comfortless, He has seperated some people for this very time we are in now. How do we know we are fully ready for a new life? But why are we afraid of change when we had no idea about this life when we first came here? We see the things around us, how they are corrupt; And even if we close our eyes they're still there. We endulge in the corruption because it's there and so tempting, yet we still want to take hold in faith. People take light to thought of good foundational truths, and hold onto things that are vain and improper. If you play people, God warns us that we reap what we sow, but you can't play God.

God, in our later years sometimes brings us back to things we've avoided in our early years; even those years growing up as a child. He determines our capabilites and He also determines just how much or how little we can do, but sometimes we are the ones who get scared and hold back from where He's trying to take us. He shows us that His words are true by His Holy Spirit being in us and made it evident in all mankind to know and understand the things we go through are all connected to Him. But the problem is that people fight against truth rather than fighting against sin. When you avoid fighting against sin, you leave room for the devil to come in and operate, Chrisitan or not. God doesn't give lee-way for sin. He cannot being a Holy God! That means we must submit to Him and His Authority and not leave things open for our own understanding or ways and when things seem a certain way, we need to dig deep, go back and check to make sure it is the right information we are getting by comparing it to His Word and to things we are given through His Holy Spirit; Either way, people are being operated under some form of authority but satan makes them think that it's their own. If it's not the authority by where God sent Jesus to come in and show us The Authority to follow after, it is a submission to one they know nothing about. I'm sure it's all been said plenty of times how we all have a choice in life.. Well the deception is getting deeper and deeper and as it does, it tries to make the choice harder to get back on the right side of understanding. The best thing to do is dive head first, keep going and don't stop, and to remember that the longer you stroke the more natural it gets, the more natural the waves feel until you learn to get used to the waves and the sharks don't bother you either.

OPEN DOORS- A QUICK MONOLOGUE

When you leave out of the house, you turn everything off. You shut the off the light, and you close the door. Who wants to be a broken woman? There are way too many celebrities on instagram to be the next big coke bottle superstar ... So where do I fit in? Everybody on the religous side is claiming to be the next Esther, So then she is already taken. But what about Ruth? Ruth is still on the market so I think I'll be her. Well, unfortunately that is the typical attitude of today's society young and old. Wanting to be a somebody, Or wanting to be a somebody were not. Or wanting to be a somebody who is already occupied. Don't walk through any of those doors because even though they may look nice on the outside, it's just a big empty building on the inside, because we can only add up to be who God creates us to be. It never ends and is just a repeating cycle of confusion until someone steps out to the other side to say Hey! Let's end this paradox ... Well, that is supposed to be what the whole world is doing because were one, we are not individuals. We have been grafted together each in a unique style and function for the operation of one cause and that is to live for God. Our sole purpose is to live for Him and our qualities flow from knowing Him and who we are in Him. He suffices us, not the things of this world. Not even the people of this world. What's the best way to get the most money? Which car is the fastest. Is the superbowl on? What internet speed is the quickest? There's a new phone out. My show is on can we please wait until tomorrow? The kids and wife are gone and no one is home now I can grab my beer without hearing any nagging about church. The doors are still open. The doors are still open, The doors are still open! Turn everything off shut off the lights and shut the door. You'll find peace and reasoning when you finally get to the other side of thought. This society is drained by thought, but we never thought of not thinking. Is it too late to become old fashioned before computers even existed? Yes it is ... And that is why we have to shut open doors. The quickest way to selling yourself cheap is to leave any open doors. This world wants to climb up to the right door, God's speed. The problem is they won't end up where they think they will. God says if any man climbs up any other way then the solid rock which is built up on Christ, then they are a thief and a robber. Suppose you reach out your hand to someone you love and give them something so special, special enough that it requires part of the best feature you like about your body being cut off and left to look at and watch die. And then once you give it to them, they don't want it anymore and say here, you have it! Then try to mess it up even more then when it was put to death. That hurt you to have to take it off; And not only that, it was the best part of your precious body. Well we make up the body of Christ! That's a big role to take on that we aren't fit for so we need him. He is the part of The body of The Father, who sacrificed part of the best feature of His body for us.

ENCOURAGEMENT AND BRACING THE STORM

It's in our nature to want company because God saw it first.

(SCRIPTURE Gen 2:18 KJV) "And The LORD God said, it is not good that the man should be alone". And then He made Eve. From the very beginning, God has been trying to teach us discipline. It was permissible for us to be tested from the beginning and until even now! Before the fall of mankind, God saw it good that a man should not be alone. After the fall, we all whether we know it or not, try to attain the Christ-centered character that is destined for each us, because we all try to obtain perfection. Whether in circumstances, or beauty, or knowledge or anywhere in life. The problem is that some people use what they've learned in the wrong way and because of that, Jesus shows us that it is not bad to be alone in these times for God's purposes.

(SCRIPTURE Proverbs 18:1) "Through desire a man, having seperated himself, seeketh and intermeddleth with all wisdom." In other versions of the Bible, it states something different to mean being alone as a "bad thing". I know that David was a boy who tended sheep might have been alone before God would use him to slay Goliath.

(SCRIPTURE 1 Sam 17:1-58 KJV) He wasn't influenced or convinced by the persuasive words, when he was told he was too young to fight.

(SCRIPTURE Daniel 10:8 KJV) Daniel saw visions while he was alone betimes. Even if He was afraid of being thrown into the lions den, he trusted God.

(SCRIPTURE Genesis 39:20 KJV) Joseph was alone before God started giving Him prophecies and visions.

(SCRIPTURE Genesis 7 KJV) Noah had family, yet they were alone as outcasts being seperated from society that went against them and God's plans for humanity; And the list just goes on. And this, is because of the curse upon mankind. But are we really alone in the times of our seperation? Do we really believe the scriptures? Do we really believe how God shows us the fall of mankind through Eve? The monthly curse women have adapted through Eve? Well God doesn't want any of these things for us but He is a righteous God who has made a way of escape. He wants us to be seperated and conscecrated for His purposes because He wants us to have understanding and to have it good. Now we know that can't be true. Jesus, who knew no sin, was seperated for us to live after Him. Though He knew and could relate to all mankind, He knew no sin. He bore our sins for us, yet He Himself knew no sin. He is seperated and Holy and teaches us that while we are here, we are to be the same way because of mankind's state. He is our precious idol! Paul says in (SCRIPTURE 1 Corinthians 7:8 KJV) "I say therefore to the unmarried and widows, It is good for them if they abide even as I."

(SCRIPTURE Matthew 19:10-12 KJV) "His disciples say unto Him, If the case of the man be so with his wife, it is not good to marry. But He said unto them, All men cannot receive this saying, save they to whom it is given. For there are some eunuchs, which were so born from their mother's womb: and there are some eunuchs, which were made eunuchs of men: and there be eunuchs which have made themselves eunuchs for the Kingdom of Heaven's sake. He that is able to receive it, let him recieve it".

Don't ever think of yourself as nothing because you are special in The Lord that He chose you to do His will. Just as He made the flowers, He made you to shine in a specific place for Him and for His reason. Sometimes, many ideas and thoughts may come into our minds. Many in the which try to bring us into bondage again from old sins, habbits or mentalities. You may think that you have little or no control over these things but you actually do through The Power of Christ! Once you submit your soul and mind to our maker through crying out for His Holy Spirit, it is possible to do ALL things through Him, just like He tells us through His Word! God wants us to know that we are worth way more than many sparrows and that we are not in bondage again to sin and to fear (no matter what the news tells us). We don't have to react to the flesh, all we have to do is keep it under submission to Christ! He has His right hand stuck out for you when you want to accomplish His will with a genuine heart. It's only up to you to believe it. Who can save us from a world of mistakes when we try to do it our way? Say it with me, Jesus! Who can save our hearts when we go the other way? Jesus! There is nobody like Him we just must stay close to the vine and know that we will get through our seasons of storms just like He promises. We must hold on and keep His hand! When we simply believe, He can then come in and take over, but when we hold back, we don't leave room for Him to act and help us, we need His help and the problem is sometimes we think we don't and just do things but wonder why they didn't turn out well. What we do by His Holy Spirit and for His Kingdom lasts and it lasts forever! The only way we can do things the right way is by following Jesus. We only do things the best we know how but Jesus has the full answers to all of our problems and solutions for all things! The vine that has already been established is the one we only need to stem from. No man that seperates Himself for his own work prospers forever, God says apart from Him, we can do nothing! Remember, we are all one no matter how much people try and seperate themselves or distinguish through various characteristics and appearances, they still belong to God so His will will ultimately be done in there lives no matter what side of the fence they choose, but He only waits and hopes that they choose Him. And He only gives us chance after chance. He sees the comotion and chaos on this side and is helping lots through His people but it is up to man to heed the call. He wishes for all to make it and for no one to suffer but people take their own free will to abuse it and the grace of God while the devil pumps them harder and harder with things and gifts of deceit and empty promises of things pertaining only to this life. People want to be genuine, cleave to be nice, cling to be close to God, but we cannot accept the way man tells us to go about it. Some things we have to find out for ourselves. The Lord says to taste and see that He is good! Sometimes we even have a tendency to be nice to people, we know how to be nice or smile or give a good gesture. Things that we have practiced have become effortless and natural to us for The Word says (SCRIPTURE Romans 2:14 KJV) "For when the Gentiles, which have not the law, do by nature the things contained in the law, these, haveing not the law are a law unto themselves." So sometimes, people want to be nice or have a form of godliness about themselves so they will people please which is only good if you wanna please The Lord! All things are good, but not all things are expedient/ suitable to purpose. Our purpose driven life is more than that we hear, our purpose driven life is about purpose! Purpose that is not our own for our own selfish gain!

Remember your past struggles, not to be let down by them but because satan will try to use those struggles against you to hinder you from where God is trying to bring you through sin. Even though people will try to sway your thoughts from God's original plan for your life, doesn't neccessarily mean that they are trying to do evil against you. It means that each one of us have fallen short of God's glory through disobedience and we think opposite of God. People do what they think is right in their own mind but remember it is God who placed you on this earth for His purpose, not for them or not for theirs. Most times people don't know when they're being used. Whether by the enemy or by God. Once we know God, He gives us authority to know who He is and that we are being used by Him. When given His authority, we use it only according to His purpose, not our own or for our own selfish gain; and He warns us to beware of false prophets who come in sheep's clothing that outwardly appear righteous to people, but inside they are wolves seeking prey. God tells us that we will know them by their fruits. When we see the roof of a house come off and all of the parts of it on the floor, do we just assume that a tornado hit it? or do we look for what caused the roof to come off? Well, sometimes we just find some things more acceptable and tolerable in our minds so we go with what we see instead of digging into the matter. All things will be proved by God someday, and when that day comes we are gonna see alot of things start to errupt from the surface that we didn't expect or even know, maybe even care about. Now the world teaches us to go by what we feel instead of trusting in God's word, but then again we know that the world is not of God. Believing is all a part of trusting God for what He says, not trusting in mans word or self. We have to believe the Authority that God put in us because it's not us; and what

He says about us is true. When you truly deny yourself for Jesus' and the Gospel's sake, you start to see life in many ways and you start to speak not only for yourself, but whatever God has placed on you to say or do. It is God's work and it's a work more than yourself. A quality work for Kingdom purposes and not our own agendas or fleshly desires. So it's good when we can remember our struggles or weaknesses to make us stronger, but it's even better to remember the grace that was given to us for us to fully overcome them and know that each and everyday we have a fight to fight and a race to win. He gave us the strength to do it we just gotta use it.

FOLLOWING JESUS ;)

It is amazing and beautiful how Peter mimicked what Jesus did and followed Him so closely. Jesus told Peter that (SCRIPTURE Matt 16:18 KJV)" Upon this rock will I build my church" If you have ever had a child, you notice that sometimes children always try to mimmick you and do what you do. They follow down behind you too. Sometimes you don't realize that it's because they want to be just like you and because you resemble their Jesus! Children know that they need a leader and that is some of the beauty Jesus sees in children. That is why they are truly a gift from God. They know they need a leader and they are susceptible to listen to you. As adults, we tend to get the hang of life and that's it. But sometimes we forget that we need a leader too. I don't mean a leader by a man-kind figure, I mean God. When we do things the way we get used to and accustomed, we forget that it was God who showed us how to do it in the first place, not ourselves. Jesus places the ones who are closest to Him on a pedestal as an example of those whom He places closest to Him. Jesus is so precious and All-Wise, that He uses the things that we like to get our attention to Him. Once He has our attention, we can start to follow down behind Him and understand His ways. We start to see and understand life too, not in the way we were taught by man, but how He wants us to see it in our personal relationship with Him. satan uses things we like too, to try and get our attention so keep your guard up.

When we get a glance at things in this life, we get a glance at Heavenly things too; And anything that will not be burned up. I say that because in Revelation, God gives us understanding of His layout which is different from earth. At the same time they still resemble things we see and know about earth and life. That is why it says in (SCRIPTURE 1 Corinthians 7:31 KJV), how we should use the things of the world as not abusing it, because our things are stored up for Heaven. Always, when we walk like the rest of the people in the world, we start to see feel smell touch and want what is closest to us but why should we want things that aren't closest to the heart. Nothing is intangible to us, but God has to show us how to do things and at His time. It is our faith walk with Him that we have. The closest things to our heart is God, so things try to touch it and corrupt your natural character to make you chase after that thing instead of the one who gave it. Jesus wants us to chase Him and He tells us the things that will happen to us when we do it. By nature we want Jesus. Things have kept me back from knowing Jesus for so long and in so many ways the enemy has used distractions to try and base that as my personal issue when that was not. I was distracted because of my lusts and the fact that I was blind! But Jesus made a way, and makes a way for all of us!

(SCRIPTURE John 3:5 KJV) "Jesus answered, Verily, verily, I say unto thee, Except a man be born of water and of the Spirit, he cannot enter into the kingdom of God."

God is too Holy to allow man who is corruptible to enter into His divine Kingdom! He is a Holy and just Righteous God! Think of how impure this world is and the things that you hate. I bet you hate the fact that people have to die. Well God wouldn't have it that way for us. He wants us to live forever; and nothing can stop us from that very thing when were on the right path. Store up for yourselves treasures where theives don't break in and steal.

(SCRIPTURE Reference Matthew 6:20 KJV)
Store up heavenly treasures.

The devil made mankind sucseptible to draw out our own conclusions about everything in life. So when you hear people say that the devil made them do it, they're being funny but it's all true. They don't know the force behind what they are doing and don't understand it's power but they are under the influence. Nothing is evil in itself, but mankind abuses the things that God freely gives to us and makes them into things of mans own ideas which in turn makes it corrupt and it wont last (SCRIPTURE Reference 1 Co 7:31 KJV). That is a part of our carnal mindset we must eliminate and subject to the Almighty power through His Authority by His Holy Scriptures and His Holy Spirit. We didn't create ourselves, God created us all of us! Not for us to forget the simplicity that is in Jesus and base things on our own understanding. God shows us even through Peter His disciple, (when He rebuked him for coming against the plan of God which was death on the Cross,) That shows how every man is susceptible to satans schemes and how we must be diligent to follow God carefully considering all circumstances by walking as Jesus did, in His light! (SCRIPTURE Revelation 12:9 KJV) "And the great dragon was cast out, that old serpent, called the devil, and satan which decieveth the whole world: he was cast out into the earth, and his angels were cast out with him." satan made things seem as though they weren't what they are, because he learned by the ways of God, being as though he were an Angel in Heaven that got cast down; he tricked Eve into thinking that she wasn't satisfied. he may be the reason why our Lord is teaching us discipline and that without it, no man shall see our Lord. God doesn't want anything to seperate us from Him, not any desire on this earth so we must constantly strive for Him in all things!